DEVELOPING INDIVIDUAL VALUES IN THE CLASSROOM

by Richard L. Curwin, Geri Curwin
with the editors of LEARNING magazine

Fearon Teacher Aids
a division of
PITMAN LEARNING, INC.
Belmont, California

FOREWORD

Every student can come to understand who he is and how to become more like his ideal self. In this book you'll find almost 100 classroom-tested value discovery ideas, projects and activities. You'll also get some down-to-earth suggestions on how to facilitate the development of trust and self-respect in the classroom.

The purpose of this and other LEARNING Handbooks is to help make teaching and learning more effective, interesting and exciting. Richard L. Curwin is an Assistant Professor at the State University of New York, Geneseo, where he teaches value clarification and other humanistic education approaches. Geri Curwin does in-service training of teachers in humanistic education. Their extensive experience has been combined with LEARNING magazine's research facilities and editorial depth to produce this down-to-earth and lively handbook.

Editor: Karen Myers
Editorial Administrator: Carol B. Whiteley
Designer: David Hale
Photography: Phiz Mezey
Cover: Tony Naganuma

Executive Editor: Morton Malkofsky
Design Director: Robert G. Bryant

Our thanks to Lakeview Elementary School, Oakland, California, for their cooperation.

Library of Congress Number: 74-16806

ISBN-0-8224-1902-5

1. 9 8 7 6 5

CONTENTS

A friend is someone to ride bikes with.
A friend is to have birthday cake with.
A friend is to barbequing with.
A friend is to go to the movies with.
A friend is to go to school with.

1
INTRODUCTION TO VALUE CLARIFICATION

Growing up in today's fast-paced, problem riddled world is no easy task. Conflicting information comes from family, friends, school, the mass media and a myriad of other sources, presenting children with what appears to be a fragmented and sometimes threatening world. Teachers have the complex job of helping children put together the pieces in order to survive, to make wise decisions and to live as good a life as possible. Yet, traditionally, education has had surprisingly little effect on students' ability to make decisions and to find clarity in their lives.

Values are the most important influences on our lives. They make up our self-definition. Values are the highest priorities that we hold dear and precious to us. Our values guide every decision we make and perpetrate the very quality of our lives.

Value clarification helps students meet their need to find meaning and order in their social environment. It is a flexible method of incorporating the goals and procedures of affective education in the existing framework of all types of schools and classrooms. This handbook presents many value clarification activities to use in your teaching, as well as suggestions and strategies designed to help you initiate and maintain a value clarification program.

Value Defined
Our definition of a value comes from many sources. Kluckhohn says, "A value is not just a preference but a preference which is felt and/or considered to be justified — morally or by reasoning or by aesthetic judgment, usually by two or three or all of these."[1]

Machotka defines a value as an internalized set of principles derived from past experience, which has been analyzed in terms of its "morality." These principles enable the individual, during a

---

[1]Clyde Kluckhohn et al., "Value and Values Orientations in the Theory of Action," *Toward A General Theory of Action*, eds. Talcott Parsons and Edward A. Shils (Cambridge, Mass.: Harvard University Press, 1951), p. 396.

period of choice, to act with dispatch, predictability, orderliness, an awareness of the consequences and an internalized feeling of "rightness." To a degree, the individual seeks to enforce the value and "sees to it that it is observed by others."[2]

Another characteristic of a value is that it is freely chosen. Jacob and Flink state that "a value is 'authentic' when behavior is sanctioned by it rather than by external coercive sanctions."[3] Finally, a value is not a simple concept but a complex mixture of more than one factor. Shirk says a value "is not expressible as a simple, isolated noun but is shorthand for a three-sided relation which includes (1) what is preferred, which involves as well what is rejected, (2) one who prefers and rejects (that is, discriminates) and (3) the context within which this activity takes place."[4]

Raths, Harmin and Simon have developed a model of valuing that is useful in developing curriculum and in teaching. They divide the process of valuing into three parts: choosing, prizing and acting.

CHOOSING

1. A value is freely chosen.
2. A value is chosen from alternatives.
3. A value is chosen after careful thought of the consequences of each alternative.

PRIZING

1. A value is cherished. One is happy with the choice.
2. A value is prized enough to be publicly affirmed. One is proud enough of a value to make it public and has no desire to hide it.

ACTING

1. A value is acted upon, not just talked about.
2. A value is acted upon repeatedly. It is a pattern of life.[5]

In this handbook we combine all the above definitions of a value into a concept of valuing, which teachers can use to help students make better decisions in self-awareness and maximize their full potential.

Value Clarification Defined

Value clarification is a process that helps students examine their

---

[2]Otakar Machotka, The Unconscious in Social Relations (New York: Philosophical Library, Inc., 1964), p. 221.

[3]Philip E. Jacob and James J. Flink, "Values and Their Function in Decision-Making," American Behavioral Scientists Supplement, vol. 5 (May 1962): 5–34.

[4]Evelyn Shirk, The Ethical Dimension: An Approach to the Process of Values and Valuing (New York: Appleton-Century-Crofts, 1965), p. 4.

[5]Louis E. Raths, Merrill Harmin and Sidney Simon, Values and Teaching (Columbus, Ohio: Charles E. Merrill, 1966), p.30.

lives, goals, feelings, concerns and past experiences in order to discover what their values are. Part of the humanistic movement, it endorses study of the self through an explicit, structured mode of self-inquiry. Value clarification teaches students a process which they can use to examine their own lives, to take responsibility for their behavior, to articulate clear values and to act in congruence with their values. Value clarification does not indoctrinate students in a pre-determined, rigid set of values.

Value Clarification for Young Children

The need for structured decision making knows no age limits. Although children are given fewer opportunities than adults to make decisions, they are nevertheless faced with several choices every day:

How shall I act?

With whom shall I be friendly?

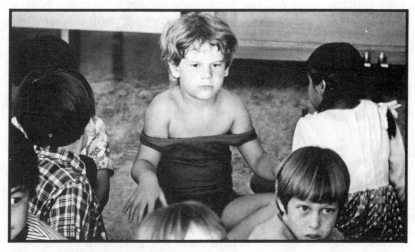

What shall I do with my time?

What games shall I play?

Whom shall I emulate?

These and other similar questions are important factors in elementary school childrens' lives. Their values are in constant flux and need to be tested and clarified as they repeatedly face certain basic questions:

Who am I?

Who will I be?

How am I changing?

Diversity must be understood, noted and discussed. Especially

7

today, children need to become more tolerant of other people's life styles and values.

Finally, children need value clarification to cope with values and decision making as they grow older. We believe that value clarification, once learned, is carried from childhood into adulthood, from your classroom into the students' future world.

The Teacher's Role

You have a three-part role in the value clarification process. First, you must provide structure for value clarification activities — supplying materials, organizing time, giving directions and facilitating interactions. Second, your actions and words must be congruent. We do not believe that teachers should "teach" their values to students. This does not mean you must be free of values or have a value neutrality — you have values — share them with your students. However, the teacher's values ought to be seen by students as possible alternatives, not as the only correct values. By showing students that values are an essential part of your life, you can validate the entire valuing process for them. Finally, you should be in the process of clarifying your own values publicly in the classroom. Sometimes this will mean that you actively participate with the students, sharing responses as a member of the group. In such cases we suggest that you respond last, so that the students not be tempted to emulate you or to oppose you.

Tell students they will be working to understand their values by doing these activities. The way you explain the process will of course depend on the age of the students. For very young children you might say, "The study of *you* is important. We will be looking at the most important things in *your* life, the way you make decisions and the feelings and thoughts that help you make choices." Older children will be able to use the word "values" in a meaningful way once you have discussed it with them and presented examples.

Establish the Proper Classroom Atmosphere

Classroom atmosphere must be built upon trust, which is explained more fully in Chapter 2. There should be a feeling of warmth and acceptance in the classroom. Differences of opinion are accepted and, in fact, desired. Students and teacher alike must be supportive of one another and sensitive to each other's needs. The curriculum must be flexible enough to deal with the individual needs of students, rather than a rigid, closed structure that is more important than the students it serves.

Students need to feel comfortable with their privacy. In value clarification we emphasize self-disclosure at whatever level the students wish for themselves. Disclosure is always voluntary. The right to "pass," to avoid participating, is inherent in all activities. Individuals are not to be pressured to explain their positions nor to defend their choice to pass. For public affirmation to be useful in the valuing process, it must be freely chosen.

There can be no explicit or implicit put-downs, insults or scapegoating. Sarcasm or insults disguised as jokes are destructive to the clarification procedure, and they undermine humanistic education. No person's growth can be gained at the expense of someone else's. Moreover, there can be no gossiping about information learned in or outside the class in a value clarification activity. Feelings and thoughts expressed by students deserve respect and care. They need to be appreciated in the same spirit in which they were given, shared by someone who is seeking to learn and grow.

Grading Students

Although the activities are generally followed by some type of evaluation procedure (see Chapter 6), there can be no grading. The evaluations are personal and done by the student, not the teacher. The teacher may, and is encouraged to, evaluate how well a particular activity is going, but this can never be translated into an evaluation of students. In value clarification there are no wrong answers, and grading would only serve to stifle trust, honesty and a willingness to self-disclose. All responses are personal and individual.

Keep It Lively

Value clarification can be a meaningful method to help your students become responsible, aware and curious individuals. Or it can become merely another segment in a predictable school day as students go through reading, spelling, value clarification, arithmetic and art. If value clarification is approached as another chore, or the students perceive it as just another "school subject" unrelated to their real lives, it will break down into a series of unrelated games which do the students no good at all. The greatest advantage of the value clarification model is that it relates to students' lives directly and inclusively. It gets at the very heart of the students' existence. If it loses this zest and vitality, it will become merely a time filler. Keep value clarification alive by being flexible, by employing real issues and ideas of students and by treating it as a human endeavor, subject to the excitement and frailty of all human endeavors.

2
BUILDING TRUST — A STARTING POINT

Few would argue with the belief that students must trust each other and their teacher, or that the teacher should trust his or her students. But just what do we mean by "trust," and how do we achieve it? It is useful to view the process of trust building in operational, sequential stages. These stages are described as separate, identifiable entities only for the sake of clarity. In actual practice they overlap and blend into a unified process. The three stages are: (1) acceptance, (2) willingness to take risks and (3) openness.

Acceptance
Acceptance is a nonjudgmental response. When you act in an acceptant manner you neither praise nor censure another person's information, opinions, behaviors or values. Being acceptant does not imply that you agree with everything, but rather that you withhold judgment while attempting to better understand a response. Some examples of acceptant responses are: "I understand how you feel, although I feel differently"; "I see how that works for you, but I prefer a different alternative"; "I appreciate your sharing your feelings with me."

Willingness to Take Risks
People who interact in an acceptant environment are not afraid to share their true thoughts and feelings; they are willing to risk self-disclosure because they know that they will neither be put down nor forced to defend their views.

Openness
We define openness as taking risks of self-disclosure by sharing true thoughts and feelings. Openness flourishes in an acceptant environment; as you are open with others, they will be more open with you. Trust comes when you are being acceptant of others, willing to risk self-disclosure and, finally, being open about your thoughts and feelings with others.

Learning to trust yourself involves the same basic pattern. As you become more acceptant of yourself, you will be able to take more risks and, finally, be more open with yourself about your own thoughts and feelings. You can learn to trust yourself by experiencing more trust in others, just as you can learn to trust others by experiencing more in yourself.

We find that self-disclosure[1] in a proper environment, such as an open and acceptant classroom, leads to personal growth and positive feelings. Many of the value clarification activities in this book lead to self-disclosure. It is important, however, that the student always has the option to reject self-disclosure; he may choose not to participate in every activity. Otherwise the support in the classroom will dissolve into threat.

As students become more willing to take risks, therefore building trust, they will be better able to decide whether or not to share their feelings publicly. Their decisions will almost always be in their own best interests.

In the activities that follow, the level of risk increases gradually. Because the focus of these activities is trust building, the risk is never great and the sharing of information is usually fun. The consequences of sharing are positive, with very little chance of anyone being hurt.

We suggest that you begin with the activities in this chapter, doing one each day or perhaps every other day. Building trust takes time — but these activities alone will not do the job. In addition, you must be a model of an acceptant, risk-taking and open individual. A supportive atmosphere, too, must be consciously and consistently maintained, not just in the activities, but in the daily interactions of your class.

Activity #1: Who Are We Inventory
FOCUS:
The "Who Are We Inventory" is a simple, nonthreatening way for both the teacher and the class to find out "who's who" in the classroom. The activity stresses the prizing process of valuing as students respond to questions concerning their values.
MATERIALS:
"Who Are We List."
PROCEDURE:
The teacher reads the following list (or a modified one) to the class.

---

[1]See Sidney Jourard, The Transparent Self, D. Van Nostrand Co., 1971, for more information about self-disclosure and personal growth.

In each case, students raise their hands if the statement applies to them. They may, of course, pass on any question, but they should be encouraged to take a risk, raise their hands and see who else in the class does the same. The teacher can set the tone by also responding.

Who Are We List

1. I like candy with nuts.
2. I like to stay up late.
3. I have flown in a plane.
4. I have been in a bus in a city.
5. I have been on a farm.
6. I have a pet.
7. I like tangerines.
8. I am the oldest child in my family.
9. I am the youngest child in my family.
10. I am the middle child in my family.
11. My grandmother or grandfather lives with me.
12. I can climb a tree.
13. I can roller-skate.
14. I have my own room.
15. I go to church on Sundays.
16. I like TV.
17. I wish I were older.
18. I wish I could fly.
19. I have nightmares sometimes.
20. I am afraid of shadows.
21. I am afraid of bugs.
22. I have been to camp.
23. I have been to a different state.
24. I have seen the ocean.
25. I can ride a two-wheeler with no hands.
26. I like the winter.
27. I like to jump in fallen leaves.
28. I have played in the snow.
29. I have a secret hiding place.
30. I like to go berry picking.
31. I once won a medal.
32. I choose my own clothes.
33. I have been on a team.
34. I have broken a bone.
35. I have had an operation.
36. I have a great-grandparent.
37. I watch cartoons on Saturday mornings.
38. I get an allowance for doing chores.

39. I make my own breakfast.
40. I know how to swim.
41. I have caught a fish.
42. I like pizza.
43. I like spinach.
44. I like McDonald's hamburgers better than my mother's.
45. I like to paint.
46. I make models.
47. I catch butterflies.
48. I can shoot a bow and arrow.
49. I love chocolate ice cream.
50. I have been to a symphony concert.
51. I like to dress up.
52. I have a library card.
53. I like rock 'n roll.
54. I can dance.
55. I like my middle name.
56. I have been to a professional ball game.

FOOTNOTE:
The reading and hand raising should take about fifteen minutes. There are, however, many possibilities for expanding this list into discussion and further activities. You may wish to pause along the way and let students add statements of their own. Or students may wish to create their own lists for use throughout the year.

Activity #2: Name Poems
FOCUS:
"Name Poems" lead students through the process of choosing and prizing values. The students create banners to represent themselves to the class. The banners can be worn or hung from their desks.
MATERIALS:
Construction paper, crayons, recycled magazines, scissors and paste.
PROCEDURE:
Provide each student with materials. With their names spelled vertically down the left side of the paper, they are to find (or draw) a picture whose subject matter begins with the corresponding letters of their name. Once all banners are completed, students can tour the room and "read" the name poems of their classmates.
Example:
J   (picture of someone jumping)
I   (picture of ice cream)
M   (picture of a motorcycle)

FOOTNOTE:
Children with adequate vocabularies and writing skills can use words alone or words in addition to pictures. You might even ask for rhymes or parallelisms.

Example:

J   jumping
A   arguing
M   mimicking
E   eating
S   smiling

Activity #3: Getting To Know You

FOCUS:
This activity serves three purposes. First, it gives students a chance to exchange ideas and information and to establish lines for further communication. Second, it gives the entire class a chance to learn about each class member. Third, it gives the students an opportunity to appreciate the need for good listening.

MATERIALS:
None.

PROCEDURE:
Pair off each student with another student; avoid pairing students who already know each other well. Let each pair find a space to speak without interference from other pairs. Give them five to seven minutes (longer for older children) to talk about themselves. Younger children may need some guidelines or suggestions for things to talk about, such as hobbies, sports, favorite television shows, pets, school and home life. After the time limit is up, bring the group into a large circle with each student sitting next to his or her partner. Then have each student in turn speak to the large group about his or her partner. The student can begin, "This is my new friend (*partner's name*), and he/she . . . ," finishing with items from their discussion. While one student has the floor, no one else should be allowed to speak. After everyone has had a turn to speak and be spoken about, the teacher can moderate a question and answer period. Of course, each student has the option to pass.

FOOTNOTE:
If the number of students is uneven, the teacher may become a partner and participate in the activity.

Activity #4: Scavenger Hunt

FOCUS:
The "Scavenger Hunt" is an inventorying activity that focuses on

choosing and prizing values; it is designed for small group work.

MATERIALS:

"Scavenger Hunt List" for each student.

PROCEDURE:

The class is divided into groups of four or five students. Each group is given a list of items to "find" on their scavenger hunt. In addition, the students are to name something that they *all* like and something that they *all* dislike under each category. They receive one point for each consensus they reach. (Each group will need a secretary to keep score.)

Scavenger Hunt List

	Like	Dislike
1. food		
2. game (indoor)		
3. TV show		
4. game (outdoor)		
5. gift received		
6. summer vacation		
7. school subject		
8. chore at home		
9. hobby		
10. a way to spend a Saturday		

In the second half of the activity, students "search" for experiences they have had in common. They receive three points for each experience they decide they have all had.

Examples:

1. a time when their parents made them very happy
2. a time when they were uneasy in school
3. a time when they felt left out
4. something they have done with their friends about which they're proud
5. a time when they got away with something they shouldn't have

FOOTNOTE:

The teacher must stress honesty in all discussions. A suggested time limit for the activity is 30 minutes. Once the groups have completed the "Scavenger Hunt," they might choose two items to share with the entire class, perhaps those ideas that were most fun or most difficult. Then the scores from both activities should be added to determine which team accumulated the most points.

Activity #5: I'm The Same; I'm Different

FOCUS:

This activity lets students see how they are like and unlike other students in the class. It is primarily concerned with the presentation of alternatives. The object of the activity is to give each student a chance to discover that he or she is unique. When this happens, he is considered "out," participating only by submitting blank pieces of paper.

MATERIALS:

Pencils and paper.

PROCEDURE:

Form the class into a large horseshoe with you at the opening of the semicircle. Have each student tear a piece of paper into eight pieces, using four and saving four for later. Students start by finishing the sentence, "I'm different, special, unique, unlike others because . . . ." They do this with each of the four slips of paper, writing something truthful about themselves that they feel will set them apart from the rest of the class. What they write can be either positive or negative; it can be related to their feelings, thoughts, hobbies, problems, relationships or schoolwork. *It is important that the students understand that this information is anonymous and that no one will identify them with what they have written.*

The teacher then collects one slip of paper from each student, shuffles them and reads them aloud. Instruct students to raise their hands if a statement applies to them, but not to raise their hands for their own statements. In most cases, each slip will evoke a number of raised hands; when no hand is raised it means that the information on the paper applies only to the person who wrote it. Thus the writer of that statement is unique or different from the class and is "out," but he never has to identify himself to the rest of the class.

Once you have completed this procedure, explain to the class that they will have another chance to become unique. They may either submit another slip on which they have already written, or use one of the blanks to write something new. Proceed as above. All students should submit a piece of paper each round—a blank one if they are already "out." Do as many rounds as necessary to let each class member experience being unique.

FOOTNOTE:

This procedure is complicated in description but not in practice. It might help if you try it once or twice with family or friends before using it in your classroom. Pre-readers can do the activity by having each student in a circle take a turn naming something that is unique to him or her. The rest of the class then raises their hands if they agree with the idea suggested. The anonymity is lost, but we find that younger children do not need it.

Here are several questions and answers that other teachers have wanted to know about this activity.

1. *Do I read every response, even if it is insulting, extremely personal or off-color?* We find that it is best if all responses are read. Rarely does a student submit anything too personal. The off-color statements test class and teacher reactions. When they're treated as valid responses, students no longer respond in this way. Of course, your own judgment should be the deciding factor.

2. *Once a student is "out," can he submit more slips of paper?* Yes, this can be allowed; it keeps students interested if they get "out" early.

3. *How long should the game last if there are only a few who are not "out"?* Give students every possible opportunity to get "out." It is important to their self-image, even if other students become a little bored.

4. *Should I allow cop-out answers, such as, "I have a planter's wart on my big toe"?* While this answer may not reveal a personal aspect of a student, it provides a safety valve for those who are not yet ready to take bigger risks, and it helps those get "out" who are unable to think of a better answer. We suggest those answers be discouraged but accepted.

Activity #6: Personal Collage

FOCUS:

This activity develops the value processes of choosing and prizing. Students think about different answers to the question "Who am I?"

and share their answers visually. "Personal Collages" also help class members practice acceptance of one another.

MATERIALS:

Scissors, glue, tape, construction paper and recycled magazines.

PROCEDURE:

The teacher gives supplies to each student. Students then complete the statements that follow this paragraph by making a personal collage, descriptive of their answers. Once the collages are finished, they may, if students wish, be placed on walls or bulletin boards around the room. Or, each student can make a presentation, showing his collage to the class, explaining the significant aspects and verbally completing the statements. Remember that a student may explain his position, but he must never be forced to defend it.

Suggested Collage Completions

1. Favorite things I own are. . . .
2. I love to. . . .
3. I want to become. . . .
4. A typical afternoon for me is. . . .
5. If I could go anywhere, I would go to a place like. . . .
6. Sometimes I feel like. . . .
7. I want to learn how to. . . .
8. I have trouble with. . . .

Activity #7: Highest Bidder

FOCUS:
In this activity, students have a chance to examine their priorities and make choices on the basis of those priorities. Students will work in groups, learning how to make effective group decisions; they will begin to understand the role of personal priorities in determining group priorities.

MATERIALS:
"Auction List."

PROCEDURE:
The class is divided into groups of three or four students who are not close friends. Each group gets a copy of the "Auction List" and 150 fatons (bogus currency unrelated to money). Explain to the students that each item will be auctioned off in order of its appearance on the "Auction List" to the highest bidder. Once a team runs out of fatons, its members can no longer bid. No individual can make purchases, nor are the fatons given to individual students.

Once the auction is completed, give the class a chance to discuss what they received, what they wanted and didn't get and what their group purchased, even when one member might not have approved. Let the students make up their own list for the next auction.

Auction List
1. $1,000 for each member of the group to spend in any way wanted
2. a perfect report card for an entire year
3. a free, all expense paid trip to Disneyland, the World Series or a rock concert with anyone of your choice
4. a chance to spend a day with your favorite TV character
5. ten minutes in a store of your choice, collecting whatever you can cart out in a wheelbarrow
6. a perfect back yard, filled with every toy, game or amusement that you can imagine
7. a guarantee that you will become President of the United States when you are older
8. a week in which no one can tell you what to do
9. a chance to run your school for a week
10. a perfect vacation for your parents — they can go wherever they want and do whatever they want for a week, at no cost to them or to you
11. perfect health for your entire life
12. a chance to become the most beautiful or most handsome person in your entire community
13. the opportunity to eat whatever you want for one year

14. the chance to personally solve the world's pollution and environmental problems

15. the promise to have a perfect friendship for life — your friend will be exactly what you want him or her to be

FOOTNOTE:

Remember that the group buys each item but each member of the group gets the complete item. Make sure you have time for discussion at the end of the activity because it is extremely important. For students who are unable to compute, prepare faton certificates and personally take away the necessary amount for what they have bought. It is also helpful to make picture cards of the items and give them to the group that buys them. Keep a chart on the board, naming the items and the selling prices. This activity works best when the teacher gets into the spirit of auctioning and hams it up, instilling the spirit in the students. Keep trying to raise the price, but don't dwell too long on any one item.

Activity #8: Group Composite Drawing

FOCUS:

Students examine their priorities concerning selected topics and interact in a group situation, sharing, compromising and learning with other group members.

MATERIALS:

Large sheets of drawing paper or newsprint, and crayons, paints or other picture making supplies for each group.

PROCEDURE:

Divide the class into small groups of about five or six students, and give each group one blank sheet for each of the topics listed below. Each group is to draw a picture expressing the group's response to each of the topics. Emphasize that the entire group must agree to every aspect of the drawing; the students cannot select by majority vote. Each student should also have a chance to participate in the actual drawing of the picture. Once the pictures are completed, each group can display its work, explain it and then entertain questions from the class as a whole.

Picture Topics

1. a composite of games
2. an ideal bedroom
3. an invention that is a form of transportation
4. a fictional new kind of pet
5. a robot
6. a tracing of an actual group member's body on a large sheet of paper and then choosing features and details from other group

members to add on to the outline, such as Susan's hair style, John's feet, Paul's sweater, Mary's eyeglasses, etc.

Activity #9: The Detective Game

FOCUS:
Every child possesses certain articles that identify him as an individual. In this activity, children can play detective to establish the identity of someone in the class through material possessions. Students sharpen their powers of observation and also select something they own to represent them.

MATERIALS:
A personal item belonging to each child.

PROCEDURE:
One child is chosen to be the detective. He or she leaves the room while all the other children, except for one child, select an item from

their person, desk or locker to represent them, and put it in a central location. The idea of the game is that an alleged crime has been committed by the student who didn't leave a clue. It is the detective's job to carefully examine all of the clues (the possessions of the students), making use of his knowledge of these students and their possessions and matching up belongings with owners. When he returns the items to their owners, he must explain why he believes a specific clue belongs to a specific person. He is to return all the clues to the rightful owners, thus determining the student who did not leave a clue, the one who committed the crime. Once he makes a mistake, the detective is "out," and the game must be started again with a new detective and new clues.

FOOTNOTE:
The clues should not be obscure, that is, a pencil or textbook wouldn't be an acceptable clue. Each clue must be recognizable. Some examples might be a drawing someone has done (with the name withheld) that has been on display, a toy someone has brought in for show and tell, a jacket someone wears regularly to school or a ring someone has had on recently.

Activity #10: Imagine Me . . . Imagine You
FOCUS:
"Imagine Me . . . Imagine You" leads students to think divergently about themselves and others. Students perceive various aspects of their personality in a rather light, unusual manner.
MATERIALS:
"Imagine Me . . . Imagine You List" for each group.
PROCEDURE:
Divide the class into circles of four or five students. Going around their small circles, the students will share how they see themselves and every other group member in terms of the list. They will also state as specifically as possible why they feel as they do. Once all have spoken, using two or three items from the list at a session, the students are to choose the most interesting statement they made about themselves and the most interesting statement they heard about themselves and share these statements with the entire class. Students might even draw a picture of the two responses about themselves for a bulletin board display. Naturally, some categories will be more appropriate to your students than others.
Imagine Me . . . Imagine You List
1. "Imagine me . . . Imagine you": as an animal
2.   ″   ″   ″   ″   : as a holiday
3.   ″   ″   ″   ″   : as a kind of food

4. "Imagine me . . . Imagine you": as a kind of TV program
5. " " " " : as a part of nature (other than animal)
6. " " " " : as some object in the classroom
7. " " " " : as a kind of building
8. " " " " : as some kind of vehicle
9. " " " " : as a member of some "grown-up" profession
10. " " " " : as a kind of game
11. " " " " : as a piece of geography
12. " " " " : as a piece of playground equipment
13. " " " " : as a kind of school lesson
14. " " " " : as a season
15. " " " " : as a color

FOOTNOTE:
Students should be reminded that they are considering personalities and not likes, dislikes or similarities. This type of figurative thinking may be new to your students; give them some examples to get them started. Emphasize that although it is fun to imagine these things, they should try not to be silly. Although no writing is involved, this activity is probably not suitable for fairly young children.

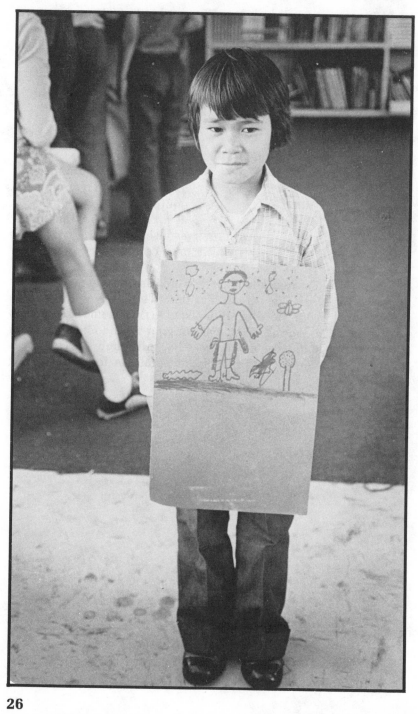

3
HELPING CHILDREN DISCOVER THEIR TRUE SELF

Most teachers begin to see signs of acceptance and openness in their classrooms after some initial work with activities designed to build trust. While there is no magic turning point punctuated by firecrackers and pealing bells, there will be subtle signals from students who are developing trust toward one another and toward you. If the signs of trust are there, and if you recognize them when you see them, move on to the value clarification activities in this chapter.

These activities have been divided into two separate but related themes. Part 1 presents activities that help students focus inwardly. These activities cover a wide range of personal concerns and lead students into the process of self-discovery. Part 2 contains activities that focus outwardly. Here, students will develop deeper understanding about the way they relate to others — family, friends or others who have significance in their lives.

The activities in each part proceed from the simple to the more complex. Activities toward the end of the chapter often involve several steps and require students to probe more deeply into personal material.

While all activities can be performed separately, we believe that they work best in the order suggested. You, however, must be the final judge about which activities to use and which order to follow. Omit those that have little or no meaning for your students. Adapt other activities so that they better fit your classroom. Expand those that are particularly successful.

Because of the nature of the activities in this chapter, we have added a set of directions for each. This step-by-step guide outlines your role, as well as the students' participation. Directions and questions for each activity can be modified at any time. Remember that the examples and activities were written for a wide general audience — only you can make them suit your own students. Some activities call for students to read and write; these activities, however, can often be adapted for nonreaders as you substitute oral activity for written words. Some activities can be adapted to call for more sophisticated skills. The important thing to remember is to encourage the activities and topics that bring forth the best response in you and in your students.

After you have attempted an activity or two, you may want to keep a journal. Note the concepts, activities, examples and directions which seem difficult for students, as well as those which are easily understood. Notice what the students enjoy and attack with vigor, and which activities seem a chore. Keep notes about how long each activity takes and whether or not you needed more time for discussion. The notes will help you plan and modify future activities for your students; when you begin creating your own activities, the information will prove most valuable.

One more suggestion: Because evaluation is a central part of value clarification, we strongly urge you to read this chapter and Chapter 6 in its entirety before introducing any of the activities to your class.

PART 1
Activity #1: Feelings Vocabulary
FOCUS:

In order to do the activities in this handbook, your students need to recognize many different feelings, to understand what those feelings mean and to practice ways of expressing them. Young students, even at the kindergarten level, can comprehend and use vocabulary about feelings, and bring this vocabulary to other value clarification activities. This activity and the one that follows begin the process of building a "Feelings Vocabulary."

MATERIALS:

Large (magazine) pictures of people doing different activities and showing different emotions; camera and film (a Polaroid is the best kind, although any camera will do).

PROCEDURE:

There are several sequential steps to this activity. Students will progress from acting out simple words to identifying feelings in pictures, and finally to looking at pictures of themselves and identifying their own feelings.

DIRECTIONS:

1. The class lists three or four ways they can feel inside (i.e., happy, sad, alone or angry).

2. Different students take turns showing how their faces would

look if they felt like the words on the class list.

3. Have the students show by acting (without words) how it feels to be happy, sad, etc. Each student should use his whole body.

4. Have the class take turns making sounds (not words) that represent the words on the list.

5. Have the students show what it's like to feel happy, sad, etc., using only their eyes, hands, mouth, arms, feet or legs.

6. Acting in slow motion, have the students use their whole bodies to show what it feels like to be happy, sad, etc.

7. Read the students a story that involves feelings, or let the students read their own story.

8. Have the students role-play different characters from the story.

9. In small groups or in one large circle, have the students use the new words referring to feelings to discuss:

    a. "What happened before school today that made you feel . . . ?"

    b. "What has happened in school lately to make you feel . . . ?"

    c. "What has happened at home lately to make you feel . . . ?"

10. Ask the class to look at some large pictures depicting emotions and answer the following questions about them:

    a. "What are the people in these pictures thinking?"

    b. "What are the people hoping for?"

    c. "What happened just before this picture took place?"

    d. "What might happen next?"

11. Have some students role-play situations from the pictures, acting out what might happen next.

12. You or another student take some pictures of each student interacting in a class situation. (It might be helpful to take pictures before you begin this activity, so that you will have them ready at the proper time.) Looking at the pictures, have the students answer the

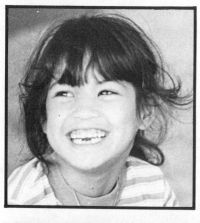

questions from step ten about their classmates, noting each time when a word referring to feelings is used.

13. Have the students answer the same questions when they see pictures of themselves.

FOOTNOTE:

This activity is long and needs to be taught over a period of time, but, since new words can be added periodically, the activity doesn't need to end before other activities are taken up by the class. The procedure we've described is applicable to any age student, although older children might have more success writing and discussing the questions.

To avoid repetition, keep a record in your classroom of words students have included in the "Feelings Vocabulary." Students who can write might wish to keep individual lists. By the end of the activity the students will have a better understanding of what feelings are and how specific words can express these feelings.

Activity #2: My Scrapbook of Emotions

FOCUS:
In this activity, your students can become more sensitive to their emotions while they find out if there is any flexibility in their feelings.

MATERIALS:
A loose-leaf binder, loops or brads; punched paper, crayons, paints.

PROCEDURE:
Your students will maintain a record of their feelings for perhaps an entire term. After they have completed the initial drawings for their scrapbooks, they will be encouraged to make changes in the positions of pages throughout the term. Finally, they will be asked to look back on these changes and discuss what implications they may have had on their lives.

DIRECTIONS:
1. Ask each student to complete this sentence ten different ways: "For me, happiness is . . . ," being as specific as possible.
2. On separate sheets of punched paper, have students draw a picture of their answers to question one (no words allowed). You might help students by saying, "If happiness for you is recess, you might draw a picture of some kids playing stickball or climbing on a jungle gym."
3. Direct students to make a title page for the "For me, happiness is . . . ." section.
4. Ask students to complete this sentence five different ways: "For me, loneliness is . . . ."
5. On separate pieces of punched paper, ask students to draw a picture of their answers to question four (again, no words allowed). Then, have them make a title page for the "Loneliness" section.
6. Repeat the procedure, completing each of these sentences five different ways: "For me, frustration is . . . ." and "For me, fear is . . . ." (Students will then have two more title pages to make, each followed by five drawings.) If students need examples, you might say, "If you feel frustrated when you do arithmetic, draw a picture of a math quiz. Or, if you're afraid of kids making fun of you, you might draw a picture of people pointing and smiling at you. For loneliness, you might have a picture of you looking out of a rain-splattered window."
7. Have students keep their scrapbooks throughout the term. Tell them, "If you change your feelings and therefore your values about certain drawings, you may move them within the scrapbook. For

example, if you're doing poorly in arithmetic but later begin to do well, you might want to move your 'frustration is math' drawing into the 'happiness' section."

8. At the end of the semester, have the class discuss or report any changes that have occurred and any deletions or additions that could be made in their scrapbook.

QUESTIONS FOR DISCUSSION:
1. Did you make many changes?
2. Did any patterns seem to emerge?
3. How flexible are your feelings? Can you answer this question by saying, "I learned that my feelings . . . ."?

FOOTNOTE:
Students can add different sections to their scrapbooks as new feelings come up, possibly from other activities. In this way, the scrapbook also becomes a record of student progress in value clarification.

Activity #3: Values Box

FOCUS:
The "Values Box" can help students discover and clarify values related to their feelings about themselves. Here, they gather symbols of their values and present them to the class.

MATERIALS:
Two small boxes for each student, crayons and paints. Use boxes about the size of a shoe box or hatbox.

PROCEDURE:
The students will use the two boxes to gather different objects that symbolize the students' values. They will then show the contents of their boxes to the class, explaining the meaning of the different objects.

DIRECTIONS:
Give students the following directions:
1. Label one of your boxes "Me" and one box "Not Me."
2. Design or color your boxes any way you choose.
3. In the next week or two, collect some objects that show what you strongly believe in and put them in the "Me" box. If you believe in:
   a. luck or superstition, you might include a rabbit's foot or four leaf clover.
   b. being rich someday, you might include a coin.
   c. religion, you might include a religious object.
   d. creativity, you might include an original poem or drawing.
4. In the "Not Me" box, collect items that represent what you do not believe in, using the same procedure as for the "Me" box.

5. There are no limits to the items you may include in your boxes.
6. After the boxes are filled, you will each have a chance to show the class what you have collected and tell what each item means.

QUESTIONS FOR DISCUSSION:
1. How difficult is it to determine what you believe in?
2. Do you think what you put in your boxes might change in the next year? How?
3. During the collection period, have you acted in any way that reflects any of the values in your "Me" box?
4. Have you done anything that reflects a value in your "Not Me" box?
5. Which box was more difficult to fill? Which had more items?

FOOTNOTE:
You may wish to repeat this activity from time to time after intervals of at least a month, and then compare the results. With younger children, you may wish to provide more examples as a guide. Older children like to be creative and usually don't need many examples. If your classroom is designed for it, you may wish to have a "Values Box" center where each student can keep his boxes semipermanently, adding things or removing them throughout the year. In this way the "Values Box" records changes over time for students and teacher to observe.

Activity #4: My Ideal Birthday Party

FOCUS:
This activity allows students to create personal fantasies which clarify their feelings and priorities.

MATERIALS:
Paper, pencil, construction paper, crayons, scissors and glue.

PROCEDURE:
Students will design an ideal birthday party for themselves. While the design of the party is private, encourage the students to share their completed creations to note similarities and differences. You will probably need to explain the concept of "ideal," as opposed to that of "real." Explain to students that there are to be no restrictions placed on them in terms of cost, feasibility, structure, guest list, etc. They may be asked to share, but never to justify, their design.

DIRECTIONS:
Give students the following directions:
1. Make a written guest list. Remember there are no limitations on the number of people or the possibility of certain guests coming. You may invite people who are no longer living, such as George Washington, or fictional characters from books or movies. You must

decide if your parents are to attend.

2. Draw a picture of the location of the party; the place need not actually exist. For example, you may have your party on a planet in outer space or in an underwater hideaway.

3. Write a list of the menu items, perhaps including some drawings of the food you want. You may choose one theme (such as an Italian dinner), a medley of your favorite foods or your guests' favorite foods.

4. Make a diagram of the seating arrangement for the meal, if that fits within your overall design. Decide who will sit near you and who will be near the other guests.

5. Write an explanation of the focus of the party. Define the activities as specifically as possible. Also include a representative drawing of the main theme (baseball game, movie, rocket ship ride or whatever). If there are games to be played, list and describe them.

6. Make a list of "ideal" gifts your guests might bring. You may include drawings of these gifts.

7. Make a list of the favors or prizes, if any, that you will provide for your guests. You may include drawings of these items.

8. Share your "ideal birthday party" plans or any part of them with the class.

QUESTIONS FOR DISCUSSION:

1. What can you do to make your next birthday party more like

your ideal one? (Students may need an example, such as, "If someone chooses to take himself and his guests to the World Series and this is not a real possibility for him, how could he include sports or baseball in his next party?")

2. How different is the party you have created from any you have ever attended?

3. Can parties be fun even if they aren't terribly unusual or spectacular? What can you do to make your next party more fun?

4. How does it feel to be the host or hostess at a birthday party? What do you do when you receive a gift you already have, or one you don't like? How might you be a better host or hostess next time?

5. How does it feel to be a guest at someone else's party? What is it like to go to a party and know only the birthday person? What can you do to feel at ease with all of the other guests? What might you do to be a better guest the next time you're invited to a party?

Activity #5: Boiling Point

FOCUS:
Often we get angry and temporarily lose control of ourselves. But it's possible, through practice, to use anger in productive ways, or at least to be less destructive. The first step is to gain awareness of how we act when we're angry and what produces the greatest anger in us. Then we can determine alternative behaviors and, through practice, exhibit them in heated moments. This activity is designed to help students become more aware of their anger.

MATERIALS:
A "Boiling Point List" for each student.

PROCEDURE:
The students will rate different situations that arouse anger, role-play these situations and reevaluate their ratings. They will then examine how they show anger in real situations.

DIRECTIONS:
1. Have students rate each item on the "Boiling Point List" from one to five, using the following key:
   (1) I get extremely angry in this situation.
   (2) I get mildly angry in this situation.
   (3) I get irritated in this situation, but not very angry.
   (4) This situation only slightly bothers me.
   (5) This situation does not anger me at all.

2. Ask for volunteers to role-play each situation on the "Boiling Point List," showing how they handle their anger.

3. Have the students reevaluate their rating scales after the role-playing.

QUESTIONS FOR DISCUSSION:
1. Did your ratings change? How much? Did they stay the same? Do you want them to stay the same or change?
2. If your ratings changed, what caused these changes?
3. Rank the situations from the one causing most anger to the one causing least anger. What do those at each end of the ranking have in common? How are they different?

Boiling Point List
1. when someone tells on you
2. when you try out for something and don't get it
3. when your friends do something without you
4. when you want to play with your friends but you have to go visiting with your family

5. when someone borrows something of yours and breaks it
6. when you want to do something and no one wants to do it with you
7. when you are unjustly accused of something
8. when you lose money
9. when you do something good and no one notices
10. when someone causes you to get in trouble

FOOTNOTE:
This exercise could be adapted for younger children by reading each item on the "Boiling Point List" to them.

Activity #6: Where Do I Live?

FOCUS:
Where you live—your country, state, town or city and residence —influences the way you form a concept of who you are. By looking at the places in which they live from a fresh viewpoint, students may also see themselves with fresh perspective.

MATERIALS:
Paper and pencils.

PROCEDURE:
The students will create a list of the places where they live and discover a personal value represented by each place. They will then act to improve each place listed, according to their individual values.

DIRECTIONS:
1. Have each student list on a sheet of paper as many answers as possible to the question "Where do you live?" Complete sentences are not necessary. Most students can usually think of at least ten answers and often as many as 20 or 25. Some examples are: U.S.A., 54 Main Street, a small town, Chicago, Alabama, a red house, the room on the second floor, a messy room, a blue room or a house with a big yard.
2. After each place on the list, have the student write, when possible, a value or quality that he has in common with the place. These can be metaphorical qualities. Some examples are: (1) a red house—value: colorful—I like to be colorful; (2) U.S.A.—value: freedom—I value my personal freedom; (3) messy room—value: casualness—I like to be casual. If the students are unable to think of a connection, they may leave some items blank.
3. Have the students share their favorite connections with the class.
4. Have the students add, next to each item on their lists, one specific thing they can do to make that place reflect their values even more clearly. These need not be large or elaborate tasks, but simple, viable alternatives. An example might be a red house—

make it more colorful by planting bright flowers or washing off dingy areas.

FOOTNOTE:
Self-contracts (see Chapter 6) are a handy format for the last part of this activity. Students can fulfill one contract each week until the list is complete. You might choose a time each week for the students to report on which contract they have fulfilled. Make sure students understand that any changes they make in the places they live should reflect their own values, not other people's ideas.

Activity #7: Newspaper of the Self
FOCUS:
This activity asks the question "Who am I?" and gives students a chance to develop many different levels of answers.

MATERIALS:
Large pieces of blank newsprint and marking pens.

PROCEDURE:
The students write a newspaper that serves the same function of any newspaper—to provide readers with information about what's happening. The "Newspaper of the Self," however, focuses on the individual writing the paper. The assignment, therefore, is to create a newspaper that reflects what is important, what is happening to and what is of value to the writer. It is essential that students have adequate time to conceptualize their "Newspaper of the Self."

DIRECTIONS:
1. The newspaper is divided into traditional sections and is set up in the recognizable format of most dailies.
2. Have the students complete each section of their newspaper by writing articles, drawing cartoons or creating features similar to those found in any local paper.
3. The following list of sections may be included:
   a. The logotype—what will be the name or trademark of the paper? (Students might want to consider anagrams or alliteration.)
   b. The news—these stories will reflect what is happening and has recently happened in the student's life.
   c. The features—the hobbies, books, movies or TV programs the student enjoyed or didn't enjoy. What personal meaning do they have? How do they relate to the student as an individual?
   d. Comics—what funny things have happened to the student recently? These may be shown in comic strip format.
   e. Sports—in what games is the student currently involved? These do not have to relate only to sporting events. Perhaps the student is in competition with a brother for the right to choose a

television show on Wednesday night. This can be translated into a sports story.

f. Editorials—what strong opinions does the student have about the way things are going for him? What actions are called for? A satirical cartoon might be appropriate for students who are capable of making one.

g. Classified section—what is the student selling or buying? What has he or she lost or found? For example, "Wanted—a friend to play Monopoly with after supper, must know rules of the game." Or, "Lost—a little bit of honesty, when I told my brother that Billy broke his model. I really broke it."

4. Students may make their newspaper as simple or complex as their ability allows. The emphasis is on insight and not on the actual product.

5. The paper may include pictures the students have drawn, photographed or cut from magazines.

6. The paper should be as up-to-date as possible. If you carry out the project over a period of time, students will no doubt be able to update items in the paper every few weeks. Each addition or change they make furnishes possible discussion material.

FOOTNOTE:
Either in small groups or with the whole class, parts or entire papers may be shared. Students should decide whether or not their papers will be read by the teacher. As an alternative or future activity, students may create a "Magazine of the Self" in the tradition of their favorite magazine. These magazines might lead to even greater diversity of expression.

PART 2————————————————————

Activity #1: Friendship Sentence Completions

FOCUS:
This is a quick, easy activity to use for introducing the concept of friendship as an area for value clarification. It provides students with a chance to consider what they value in friendship.

MATERIALS:
Paper and pencils (only needed when used as written activity); "Sentence Completion List."

PROCEDURE:
The students complete open-ended sentences about their own friendships.

DIRECTIONS:
Have the students complete the following sentences, either orally or in writing. With younger children, it might be easier to go around the room and have the entire class finish each sentence orally, before going on to the next one.

Sentence Completion List
1. I'm proud that my friends . . . .
2. I wish that my friends would . . . .
3. I'm glad my friends don't . . . .
4. I hope my friends don't . . . .
5. It makes me feel good when my friends . . . .
6. My friends are happy when I . . . .
7. I wonder why my friends . . . .
8. With my friends it's fun to . . . .
9. I might get in trouble when my friends . . . .

FOOTNOTE:
It might be best if you set aside time each day to do two or three of these completions, rather than tackling all of them at once.

Activity #2: Would You . . . .

FOCUS:
Most people would do more for a friend than they would for a stranger. However, we also have limits as to how much we will do for anyone. This activity encourages students to examine the limits that they have set on their friendships and to decide if these limits need to be modified in any way.

MATERIALS:
"Would You . . . . List."

PROCEDURE:
The students are to complete the questions on the "Would You . . . . List." After completing the questions, a class discussion or private journal writing may follow.

DIRECTIONS:
1. The students are to answer "Yes" or "No" to the questions on the "Would You . . . .List."
2. Students may wish to know how other students responded to certain questions. They might call for a show of hands on those questions.
3. A general discussion might be led by students who hold opposing views on certain questions.
4. Students are to tally the number of "Yes" and "No" answers they had in order to answer the discussion questions.

40

Would You . . . . List

Would you . . . .

1. give a friend your lunch money even if it meant you would go without lunch?
2. let a friend copy your paper and get credit for your idea?
3. take the blame for a friend who had taken someone's money?
4. remain friends with someone who had stolen your girl friend or boy friend?
5. loan a friend your bike, even if you knew no one else was supposed to ride it?
6. loan your allowance to a friend, even if he or she wouldn't tell you what it was needed for?
7. let a friend drink from your soda can, even if he or she had just gotten over the flu?
8. stop being friends with someone who turned you in for talking in class?

9. stop being friends with someone who borrowed a book from you, lost it and showed no concern?

10. continue to buy presents for a friend who never bought presents for you, even though he or she could afford it?

11. tell a friend if you didn't like a present from him or her?

12. tell a very sensitive friend that he or she has bad breath?

13. want to make friends with someone you met who lived far away?

14. remain friends with someone who has gotten involved in drugs?

15. remain friends with someone who told a secret after promising not to tell?

16. be friends with someone after your parents forbid it?

17. remain friends with someone who constantly put down your other friends?

18. help a friend make a team, even if it meant you wouldn't?

19. go to your friend's birthday party, knowing that you could go to a movie you've wanted to see with your family that same afternoon?

QUESTIONS FOR DISCUSSION:

1. If I had a large number of "No" answers, do I think I put too many restrictions on my friendships?

2. If I had a large number of "Yes" answers, do I think I am too much of a pushover with my friends?

3. Am I happy with the limits I put on my friendships?

4. What changes might I make to ensure more successful relationships?

5. Would I tell anyone about what I discovered about my friendship limits? Why might it be helpful to let that person(s) know what I learned?

FOOTNOTE:

This activity may be done with pre-readers if you use a slightly modified list and read it to them. Naturally, the discussion would be brief and more simplistic, but nevertheless important and helpful to their understanding of friendship.

Activity #3: People I Admire

FOCUS:

Most people admire others and emulate qualities they observe in others. Usually the people we most admire are those who are successful at something we would like to do well. Here students will examine qualities they admire in others to identify personal goals for themselves.

MATERIALS:

Paper and pencils.

PROCEDURE:
The students will list admirable qualities they observe in other people. They will then take steps to apply these same qualities to their own goals and behavior.

DIRECTIONS:
1. Have the students list five people they admire. Those listed must be real people, but they can be known personally or be famous people that the student has never met.
2. Next to each person's name, have the students list at least five things that make the person admirable. For example: "My Father: (1) He is considerate; (2) He is brave; (3) He buys me presents; (4) He is responsible; (5) He can be trusted."
3. The students now have created a list of qualities that they admire. Have them circle each quality that they think also applies to themselves. Have them put a star by each quality they would like to incorporate in their own lives.
4. Finally, have them list at least two things they can do to incorporate the starred items, and write a self-contract for each. Example: "Be brave: (1) Tell my mother right away when I break something. (2) Tell my friends I don't want to play when I really don't want to."
5. Later, have the students record their progress and report on their success or failure with self-contracts.

FOOTNOTE:
This activity can be done by first listing various qualities and then asking students to list people who demonstrate each quality. For example: "List three people who are creative, who are brave, who are honest or who are successful."

Activity #4: Camp Harmony

FOCUS:
This activity helps students clarify the elements that go into a friendship and some of the different values involved in friendships.

MATERIALS:
List of "Campers" for each student (see page 44).

PROCEDURE:
The students will choose from a list of possible campers those with whom they would like to spend time. From the selection process they will begin to understand how their values affect their choice of friends.

DIRECTIONS:
1. Give students the following directions:
"You are going to spend the next two weeks, day and night, at Camp Harmony. You will be forming a play group of six campers, in-

cluding yourself. You can choose who you want to have in your play group with you. Because you will be spending a lot of time together in the next two weeks, make your selections wisely. There are twelve possible campers and you must select five. The campers are:

a. Richie Money: Richie is very rich and is always ready to tell you about it. If he comes, he'll bring his color TV for his group to watch at free time, and that's the only chance you have for a TV. He might also buy snacks for the entire group with his allowance. He is used to having everything his own way.

b. Jackie Joker: Jackie is the funniest character in the group. He often makes everyone laugh with his keen sense of humor. When things get dull, you count on Jackie to liven things up. Often he makes his friends the butt of his jokes and will not hesitate to embarrass them or you for a good laugh.

c. Tillie Telltale: Tillie will always tell the truth. She will never lie to the group or hide things from them. She will never lie or hide anything from the counselors, either. She will tell if anyone breaks a rule.

d. Milty Muscles: Milty is the best athlete in camp. With him in your play group you stand a good chance of winning most athletic events against the other groups. Milty is a bully and often pushes his weight around.

e. Yolanda Younger: Yolanda is three years younger than everyone else in the group. She is easy to get along with and bright. She must be carefully supervised.

f. Lennie Leader: Lennie is the best leader at the camp. He is well respected and most people listen to him. Lennie has bad asthma and is unable to take part in any physical activities. The group might have to miss out on a camping trip if he is selected.

g. Sammy Sneak: Sammy is the most creative camper and is extremely good at getting things for the group. He will stop at nothing to help the group out, even if that means he must lie or cheat. He will let no rule stand in his way of getting something he wants for the group.

h. Ilene Informed: Ilene knows all about nature and camping. She has a wealth of knowledge and will provide the group with information about every subject. She reads a lot and spends most of her time alone. It is not always easy to have fun with her.

i. Murray Music: Murray plays the guitar well and knows a lot of songs. He will entertain the group often with his fine talent. He is homesick and must be reassured a lot. His immaturity might embarrass the group.

j. Franny Favorite: Franny knows the head counselor very well and can get special favors. She is very conceited and thinks of herself as very special.

k. Mike Moody: Mike is either very happy or very sad. When he is in a good mood, he is a good friend to everyone and fun to be with. When he is in a bad mood, he is terrible company and can be very nasty.

l. Gail Gossip: Gail has the best stories about all of the funny things that happen to everyone in the group. Now and then the funny story is about you, only then it's not very funny."

2. Have the students choose their five playmates individually.
3. Then divide the class into small groups of about four to seven.

4. Each group must choose five campers to join them, but it must be a unanimous decision—everyone in the group must agree.
5. After about twenty minutes, each group should share their decision with the class as a whole and tell how they made their selections.

QUESTIONS FOR DISCUSSION:
1. What values did each character represent?
2. Do you have any friends like those on the list?
3. Which character is most like you?
4. Would you choose different people to be classmates of yours?
5. When choosing a real friend, what values are important for your new friend to have?
6. Why is it more difficult to do this activity in a group than by yourself?

Activity #5: In My House We . . . .

FOCUS:
A child's definition of himself is derived in large part from the structure and patterns of his family. In this activity the students examine and share with others the rituals that exist in their homes. Differences in ethnic and religious backgrounds will expose the students to the variety of ways their classmates and their families observe certain events.

MATERIALS:
Large sheets of construction paper or newsprint, crayons, paints.

PROCEDURE:
There will be a general discussion of an event all students have experienced with their families, followed by individual students recalling what connotation the situation holds for them. Students will communicate their family patterns through pictures which may be shared with the class.

DIRECTIONS:
1. Ask the students to choose an event (suppertime, bedtime, first snowfall, chores, shopping, etc.) that will be familiar and interesting to the whole class.
2. Have the students consider the family rituals which are part of that specific event for them.
3. On a large piece of paper, perhaps 3' to 5' in length, ask each student to create a picture strip showing his or her family on that occasion.
4. The students are to include the people who would be present and the actions which would probably take place. Each picture need not be precise, but the natural sequence of the event is to be reflected in the placement of the pictures in the strip.
5. Once the picture strips are completed, set up a gallery where the students can tour and discover how their family's rituals are like or unlike their classmates.

QUESTIONS FOR DISCUSSION:
1. What is a ritual?
2. How important are rituals in people's lives? What function do they serve?
3. How important are rituals in your family's life?
4. How different was your family's observance from most of the other students?
5. What can you do to change your family's ritual to make it more fun or interesting?
6. What makes your family's ritual special to you? What changes would you never want made?

46

FOOTNOTE:
If your students are mature enough to understand satire, they might create comic strips, rather than serious representations of the events.

In discussion, lead students to explore the informal rituals which are practiced unconsciously in most families. If you discuss the most unusual rituals drawn by a few students, be careful to stress that these are not better, they just warrant further explanation.

Activity #6: Family Holiday

FOCUS:
Every family has values that strongly affect the family members. Often these values are reflected in the special days that the family observes. In doing this activity, the students will consider their family holidays and the values they represent.

MATERIALS:
Paper and pencils.

PROCEDURE:
The students will list different family holidays and write two or three values that each holiday represents to the family. They also will think of ways to improve each holiday and the manner in which it is celebrated. Finally, they will invent some new holidays based on other family values.

DIRECTIONS:
1. Have the students list on a sheet of paper all the holidays that the whole family celebrates together (New Years, Christmas, Thanksgiving, Passover, Fourth of July, etc.).
2. For each holiday, have the students write two or three of the typical family methods of celebration. You might say, "What things does your family usually do on that day in honor of the holiday? For example, do you have a large family meal with no time pressure? Do you give or receive presents? Do you have company? Do you sit by a fire and swap stories? Go on a picnic? Have the relatives over? Visit someone?"
3. Have the students list one or two ways that they would like to see the family celebrate differently on these holidays. (The students might take these suggestions home and test family reaction to them.)
4. The students complete their lists by thinking of the different values that each holiday represents to the family. Often these values are reflected in the manner in which the holiday is celebrated (see step two).
5. Have the students share their lists in small groups or with the class as a whole.
6. Now have each student invent one or two new holidays to cele-

brate unique family events and reflect family values. These do not have to be days that are already honored by their family. Students may use their imagination to create fantasy holidays:

    a. the anniversary of moving to a new place to live
    b. celebration of mother or father getting a new and better job
    c. celebration of a brother or sister getting into a college of his or her choice
    d. remembering and honoring the death of a pet
    e. the arrival of spring
    f. the annual summer vacation

These new holidays can reflect any event or family tradition that the students think of; however, it is best for students not to use recognized holidays that are already honored by everyone, such as the ones on the earlier list. In designing the holiday, students can include information such as the following:

    a. date
    b. name of holiday
    c. family activities
    d. the student's role in the holiday
    e. place of celebration
    f. values the holiday represents

QUESTIONS FOR DISCUSSION:

1. Which holidays are more meaningful to you, those on the first list or the ones you made up?
2. Are the values represented in the holidays celebrated during other times of the year?
3. How much influence do you have on the manner that your family celebrates its holidays?
4. Which holidays are your favorites? Which are your least favorite? What is the difference between the two?

Activity #7: Give Your Opinion

FOCUS:
Public affirmation is central to the valuing process. Yet, it might not be appropriate to publicly affirm our feelings in every situation. It is important to understand how we decide to disclose some opinions and hold back others. This activity asks students to examine their willingness to make public affirmations.

MATERIALS:
"Situation Cards" (see page 49).

PROCEDURE:
The class will consider different stressful situations in which they can choose to speak up or remain silent. They will look at their

decisions and see if they can discover any patterns in their choices.

DIRECTIONS:

1. Divide the class into small groups. Present the groups with each of the following situations and ask students to tell the group how they would respond in each situation. Groups need from 10 to 15 minutes for each situation before going on to the next.

Situation 1.

Your parents are having a discussion. It concerns whether or not you are to be allowed to sleep over at your friend's house. You are in the other room when you hear that the parent who has taken your side has said that you have had your friend sleep over many times in the past year. But that is not true. You had a different friend stay over. Would you:

    a. Not say anything at all. Let them finish their discussion and abide by their decision.

    b. Not say anything until they are finished. Then if you disagree with their decision, try to plead your case.

    c. Point out to your parents the mistake, and then let them finish their discussion.

    d. Join the discussion and try to win the most favorable decision for you.

Situation 2.

Two of your friends accidentally break a window at school during a play period. The teacher doesn't notice it until other students have gathered around the window. The teacher accuses the wrong students and proceeds to bring them to the principal's office. Would you:

    a. Tell the teacher the truth, thus getting your friends in trouble.

    b. Keep quiet and let the other students get in trouble.

    c. Try to tell the teacher that the students who were caught were innocent, but lie and say you don't know who did it.

Situation 3.

You just made a new friend and spent the afternoon playing with him. You really like his company and decide that you want to become good friends with him. The next day you overhear some other of your friends talking about your new friend. They are saying that they think he is a jerk and don't like him. Would you:

    a. Say nothing and stay friendly with both your new friend and your old friends, not playing with them all at once.

    b. Agree with them and drop your new friend.

    c. Tell them you like him and try to convince them they are wrong, even though they may become angry with you.

    d. Drop your old friends, telling them they are wrong.

Activity #8: Do You Know Your Friends?

FOCUS:

Friends are important to most of us. Yet it is surprising how much we take for granted about our friends. We make many assumptions about our friends which prevent us from knowing them deeply.

MATERIALS:

Paper and pencils.

PROCEDURE:

In this activity your students will see how well they know their friends and will begin to know them better.

DIRECTIONS:

1. Ask students to list the names of five to ten friends on a sheet of paper, leaving several blank lines after each name. Have them add the following information under each name:

   a. Write the date when you first met each friend.

   b. List three activities that you both enjoy.

   c. List two activities that you enjoy but your friend doesn't.

   d. List two activities that each friend enjoys but you don't.

   e. List the middle name for each friend.

   f. Write the name of a hero that each friend admires.

   g. Write the name of each friend's favorite television show.

   h. Write the hobby that is each friend's favorite.

The students may add any other information they wish.

2. When the list is complete, have the students go to each friend named on the list and check the accuracy of their answers. More than likely, students will have many friends in your class and you may wish to give a good deal of time to students for interviewing.

QUESTIONS FOR DISCUSSION:

1. How difficult is it to know your friends?

2. What kinds of information do you know about all your friends?

3. What do you want your friends to know about you?

4. How hard is it to ask your friends questions to get to know them better?

5. Are there some things that you do not want to know about your friends?

6. Do you have to know a lot about a person in order to be his friend?

Activity #9: Involvement Role-Play

FOCUS:

On life's stage we all act or react. We constantly choose the role we will play. If we choose to be actors, initiators of situations, we maintain control of those situations. Being reactors, relinquishing

50

control to others, seems an easier role at times. However, as reactors we must also make decisions. How involved will I become? How much will I influence the life of someone else? How willing am I to stand up for my values? This activity will expose students to hypothetical situations that will challenge their ideas about involvement. As viewers of role-play situations, as well as players, students will be asked to determine and question their involvement.

MATERIALS:
"Situation Cards" (see below).

PROCEDURE:
Students will role-play a series of situations. Although the class will know the purpose of the activity and the general situation, it is not to be informed of the specific role-play situations in advance. Only the students who perform the scenarios will know the general situation plus their particular role. In discussions which follow, most students will participate. Therefore, it is important for viewers to imagine themselves in the positions of the players during the performances.

DIRECTIONS:
1. Choose students or solicit volunteers to role-play the various situations.
2. Instruct them that they must follow the directions on the card they receive, but that they have freedom to ad lib as they please.
3. Read the class the general situation. Give the role-players time to consider what they will say and do. They are not to interact before the scene.
4. Have one scenario performed and hold the class discussion immediately following it.
5. After all of the scenarios have been performed and discussed, there might be a general discussion of the students' feelings in terms of involvement; of being reactors as opposed to actors; of protecting or exposing others; of conviction. It is here that the central issue of value clarification lies: How important are my beliefs to me? Am I willing to act on my values? Am I willing to publicly affirm my values?

Situation 1.
One morning while on the school bus, a very shy boy named Tom, who is new in town, sits next to Danny, a boy in his class. Two of the bigger boys steal Tom's hat and start to play "keep away." This upsets the driver, who demands order.
    a. Dan — you must decide how involved to become. What will you do?
    b. Tom — you must decide whether to ignore the bigger boys,

fight alone or ask for help. What will you do?

c. Driver — you must insist on order.

d. Bully 1 — you must decide how far you will go in teasing the shy boy. What will you do?

e. Bully 2 — You must decide how far you will go in teasing the shy boy. What will you do?

Questions For Discussion:

1. Have you ever been in Tom's position? How does it feel? What did you do?

2. Do you agree with the way the student who played Tom acted?

3. Have you ever been in the position Dan was in? What did you do?

4. Do you agree with the way the student who played Dan acted?

5. Have you ever been the bully? What prompted you to act this way? How did it feel?

6. Do you agree with the way the students who played Bully 1 and Bully 2 acted?

7. What purpose do "keep away" games serve? How are they harmful?

Situation 2.

The baby-sitter at Susie's house has not been told what time Susie or her sister should go to bed. The sitter calls upstairs to ask Susie and Mary Ellen what time their bedtime is. There is a special movie that both girls want to watch on television—it ends an hour after Mary Ellen's bedtime. After a discussion which the sitter can't hear, the girls come downstairs.

a. Mary Ellen — you lie and say your bedtime is when the movie ends.

b. Susie — you must decide if you'll tell the sitter the truth about Mary Ellen's bedtime or not say anything at all.

c. Sitter — you ask Susie if Mary Ellen is telling the truth.

Questions For Discussion:

1. Have you ever lied to your baby-sitter? How did you feel about that?

2. Have you ever avoided answering a question so that you wouldn't have to lie about it? How did you feel about that?

3. Have you ever been in the position where you knew someone else was either lying or purposely not admitting the truth? What did you do? How did you feel?

4. Did you ever ask someone to lie for you? What did you do? How did you feel?

5. How do you feel about the way Susie acted?

6. How do you feel about the way Mary Ellen acted?

Situation 3.

James and his best friend, Joe, go shopping at the local department store. James sees Joe take a jackknife and put it in his coat pocket. Just as they are about to leave the store, the manager pulls them aside and accuses Joe of taking the jackknife.

a. The manager — you must accuse Joe of taking the jackknife.

b. Joe — you must lie and say you know nothing about the knife.

c. James — you must decide whether to tell the manager the truth or not say anything at all.

Questions For Discussion:

1. Have you ever stolen anything? How did you feel?

2. Have you ever been with a friend who took something? What did you do?

3. Have you ever seen someone you did not know take something? What did you do?

4. Is it ever okay to steal? If so, when might that be?

5. If Joe had really wanted the jackknife and had no money, what else could he have done?

6. Has anyone ever stolen anything from you? How did you feel?

4
INTEGRATING VALUES AND CURRICULUM AREAS

There have always been a few natural teachers who, without any obvious effort, have made their subjects and courses come alive for students by giving personal meaning to the content. For most of us, however, it takes planning and practice to get such results. In this chapter, we suggest alternative methods and strategies to integrate traditional subjects—the cognitive curriculum—and the search for values.

There are three basic types of curriculum: cognitive, affective and confluent. A cognitive curriculum focuses on public knowledge—skills, information and concepts that are verifiable by many people. In contrast, an affective curriculum focuses on private knowledge—skills, insights, information and emotions that are internal. Here, each individual is the best authority on his own inner state. A confluent curriculum is one that blends public and private knowledge together into an integrated, unified approach.

An important trend in education today is the building of more integrated curricula. Mario Fantini and Gerald Weinstein[1] propose a three-tiered school. In their school, one third of the day is reserved for skills and knowledge development (public knowledge); one third for personal talent and interests (identification development); and one third for social action and explorations of self (private knowledge).

George Isaac Brown suggests a confluent approach, defined as "The term for the integration or flowing together of the affective and cognitive elements in individual and group learning sometimes called humanistic or psychological education."[2] He adds, "It should be apparent that there can be no intellectual learning without some

---

[1]Mario Fantini and Gerald Weinstein, *Making Urban Schools Work* (New York: Holt, Rinehart and Winston, 1968).
[2]George I. Brown, *Human Teaching for Human Learning* (New York: Viking Press, 1971), p. 3.

sort of feeling and there are no feelings without the mind's being somehow involved."[3]

Another approach is the third level teaching model described by Sidney Simon. He divides learning into three levels, all inter-related, where learners move freely from one level to another.

Level One: Taking in facts, basic skills and information.

Level Two: Understanding underlying concepts, structures and connections.

Level Three: Making personal meaning, value clarifying, related to self.

What these three and many other approaches to teaching have in common is the attempt to integrate learning so that neither the cognitive nor affective domain is stressed at the expense of the other. In this chapter we have selected four major curriculum areas —language arts, social studies, science and mathematics— and developed alternative lessons for each area. Because they combine the affective and cognitive domains, these lessons can be used as models and examples. You can make nearly any lesson or cur-riculum topic into a confluent one with a little imagination and an understanding of the personal needs of your students.

Language Arts Activity #1:
The What About Me Boy

FOCUS:

Language arts teachers often have textbook stories that adequately promote reading skills development but are in substance wishy-washy, irrelevant and unimportant. However, given a story with a recognizable theme or purpose, you can, with little effort. develop a list of questions to help your students clarify their values.

MATERIALS:

"The What About Me Boy" story (see page 57).

PROCEDURE:

Through discussion, get at personal meanings by asking your class to consider the value implications within it. You might employ these questions as a starting place and then move away from the story to concentrate on the theme at greater length.

DIRECTIONS:

1. Read the story aloud or have your students read it. (We have written this story as a sample. It is. therefore, more heavily value-laden than many stories you will find.)

2. Make sure your students know what has occurred in the story.

---

[3]Ibid.. p. 4.

Then go over the discussion questions that follow.

3. Next, have the class brainstorm a list of things that a "What about me child" might do to feel like somebody. Be sure to note which are positive and which are negative suggestions.

4. As a follow-up activity, have the students privately select someone they know who deserves positive attention from others, and, for a week, try to be especially kind to that person. Later they could share with the class how it felt to give to another person in that way, and what feedback, if any, they received from the person.

The What About Me Boy

It was Saturday morning and at Ronny's house that meant pancakes and sausages. Ronny jumped out of bed sniffing the good smells already making their way up to the room he shared with Stevie, his older brother.

When he got down to the breakfast table, the rest of the family was discussing the plans they had for the day.

"I'm going to take Stevie with me to the summer cottage to get things ready for the season," said Dad.

"I think Robin and I will go downtown and buy some spring shoes today. Who would have ever dreamed that a daughter of mine would have size eight feet?" Mom teased.

The twins, Gail and Gary, giggled. (It seemed they were always giggling at something.) Mom asked them what they had in mind for the day.

"It's a secret," they replied in unison.

"Well, as long as you stick close to home and don't get into trouble, I guess we'll say OK," said Dad. "But be sure you report in to Grandma if you're going anywhere on your bikes."

Together they nodded agreement.

Ronny had been very quiet while the others had shared their plans. "What about me?" he kept saying to himself, "what about me?" Ronny was the middle child. Robin, 13, was the oldest. Then came Stevie; he was eleven. The twins were six and a half. Ronny was nine and stuck right in the middle of a family that never seemed to notice him. "Ronny, what's your schedule for this beautiful Saturday?" Mom asked. "Aw, nothin'," Ronny replied.

A telephone ring interrupted their conversation; they were all so busy, and nobody ever seemed to include Ronny. Nobody really picked on him. Ronny would have probably appreciated even that kind of attention. But they were all too busy. Inside, Ronny just kept on asking, "What about me?"

Ronny was small for his age. He enjoyed sports but wasn't a very good athlete. He was always the last picked for teams at school.

There was the same old question again, "What about me?"

So, instead of looking for a ball game to join, Ronny decided to take a walk by himself. At least then nobody could leave him out. He often walked for hours in the fields behind his house, imagining himself surrounded by lots of people begging for his attention. "What about me?" they would all be saying.

He had been walking for about an hour when he noticed a small kitten in the tall grass. It was skinny and dirty with a gray coat and six toes on one foot. He picked it up, smoothing its fur. "Hey, little kitty. You're all alone, too," he said.

Ronny took the kitty home with him. He felt proud to have her, and she obviously enjoyed being held and petted. It was the first time Ronny had ever felt so special. It felt good to be needed.

When the rest of the family returned home later in the day, they all gathered around Ronny and the kitten. "Where did you get her?" "What happened to her mother?" "Have you fed her?" "Are you going to keep her?" "Can I hold her?" "Can I?" "What about me?"

Ronny answered their questions. He was glad to let the others hold *his* kitty. Oh, he still loved the kitten, but something even more important had happened that day. He was somebody. They knew it. But even more important—so did he.

QUESTIONS FOR DISCUSSION:

1. What is your position in your family? (Are you the oldest, the middle child, the youngest, the only child, a twin, etc.) Do you think that your parents treat you a certain way because of your position? How?

2. Have you ever felt like a "What about me boy or girl"?

3. What do you think it really means to be a "What about me boy or girl"?

4. When Ronny found the kitten, what did they have in common? Have you ever befriended an animal or person that was not particularly attractive, just because you had a special feeling about him or her? What happened?

5. Why do you think it was so important to Ronny to be somebody?

6. Do you need to do something or have something special, in order to feel like somebody?

7. What are some ways that Ronny can continue to be somebody to his family? What might he say to his family?

8. Often in school there are children who act a certain way, just to get attention. Are they like Ronny? How? Have you ever been one of them? What did you do?

9. Is there anybody you know that you could help feel like somebody? What could you do?

Language Arts Activity #2: Words for Me

FOCUS:
If we approach the study of words as a value-rich area, we can develop numerous ways to help students examine their values as their vocabulary grows. This activity helps students personally relate to new vocabulary words and thus have a better chance to retain their meaning and spelling.

MATERIALS:
Paper, pencils, list of new vocabulary words.

PROCEDURE:
If you make the vocabulary circle part of your weekly lesson plan, you will find that the sensitivity and honesty of your students' responses will increase as time goes on.

DIRECTIONS:
1. Have the students seated in a circle and provide them with paper and a list of new words to be learned.
2. Using the new words, have them complete in writing a sentence such as the following:

    a. (For adjectives) The last time I felt _____ was when _____ .

    b. (For nouns) A _____ is important to me because _____ .

    c. (For nouns) At my house we use a _____ for _____ .

d. (For nouns) If I had a _____ , I would _____ .
e. (For verbs) When I _____ , I feel _____ .
f. (For verbs) If I could _____ as fast (well, quietly, etc.)
as an _____ , I would _____ .
g. (For adverbs) A time to move (talk, sit, etc.) _____ is
when _____ .

3. Go around the circle asking students to share their sentences.
Ask each student his feelings about each word before moving on to
the next word.

FOOTNOTE:
As in all value clarification activities, you must respect the students'
privacy. We find, however, that most students are eager to share a
part of themselves in relation to the new words. Occasionally you
might want to have the students base a composition on one or more
of their sentences.

Language Arts Activity #3: If I Were . . . .
FOCUS:
As long as there have been schools, there have probably been
weekly composition lessons. We all can remember that first composition of the year, "What I did for summer vacation." Although
not terribly original, at least for that one assignment, we were
allowed to share something of ourselves, however superficial.
Generally, from then on, the topics were impersonal, often irrelevant. Ironically, composition assignments can be one of the best
ways to work with values.

MATERIALS:
Paper, pencils.

PROCEDURE:
A weekly lesson in composition writing can be the perfect opportunity for students to express what is important to them. Teachers
who are concerned with time restrictions need not juggle other
lesson plans to fit in value clarification activities if they just make
better use of writing assignments. The following is merely one
example of a topic. Research your students' interests and concerns
to come up with a list of other topics for composition.

DIRECTIONS:
1. Ask the students to privately rank the following in terms of
which they would most like to be.

       _____ a multi-millionaire
       _____ the President of the United States
       _____ a genius

2. For their composition lesson, ask the students to take their

number one choice and explain why they chose it. The following list raises questions for them to consider in their answer.

a. What would be the first change I would make "If I were . . . ."
b. How would I help society? How would I help my friends and family?
c. What would I do for myself?
d. What would be my overall goals?
e. Who would I ask for advice? What might I ask?
f. How would I want people to treat me? How might I change? What things about me would I hope would remain the same?

3. Students who made three different choices might be asked to read their compositions as a prelude to a general class discussion.

FOOTNOTE:
When you use composition to promote value clarity, begin with low-risk subjects and slowly move toward higher-risk topics. Never read any paper to the class without definite permission from the author. All of the activities in Chapters 2 and 3 can be starting points for compositions.

Social Studies Activity #1:
Current Events Reaction Sheets
FOCUS:
In most current events lessons, students examine daily and weekly events through newspapers, radio or television. In this activity, they respond to topical information by expressing their feelings about events, using the events to clarify personal values.

MATERIALS:
"Reaction Sheets" for each student (see example on page 62).

PROCEDURE:
Each student is given a "Reaction Sheet" which presents a current event. The student then gives a personal response to the material. Students may share their responses in class.

DIRECTIONS:
1. Prepare a "Reaction Sheet" and give one to each class member. Have the students write out answers to the questions; beginning readers can respond orally. In any case, keep the following points in mind:

a. All questions must have the word "you" as the subject. If you can rewrite the question without the word "you" and have the same meaning, the question isn't appropriate.
b. Four questions are a reasonable number. Many more on one sheet make it too much of a chore. The students can respond in words or phrases, not necessarily complete sentences.

c. "Reaction Sheets" should not be graded and no answer should be considered wrong.

d. A paragraph is the appropriate length for a response.

Sample Reaction Sheet

The governor has been quoted as saying, "Our schools are too soft. In my day we were challenged, disciplined, motivated. Today the emphasis seems to be on unnecessary things such as clubs and social activities. There must be some changes made." *The Newstar Press.*

a. Underline everything in this (article, headline story, piece, etc.) that you agree with.

b. Circle anything that you disagree with.

c. Rewrite the parts you disagree with so that they reflect your opinion.

d. How might you have felt if the story was about you?

e. What can you do at home to prove that you agree or disagree with the author's point(s)?

f. Have you ever done anything like the person in the article? What? How did it feel?

2. Students can share their responses with the entire class on a voluntary basis. This process might lead to an interesting debate,

straw voting or other activities designed to air differences of opinion.
3. Distribute and discuss "Reaction Sheets" about once a week.
Have students save their responses; in about six months, have them
reconsider the items and compare the two sets of answers to see if
thoughts have changed.

FOOTNOTE:
Almost any topic can be used on a "Reaction Sheet." It is helpful
to keep a file of interesting and controversial articles. As you read
a newspaper or magazine, cut out articles that have promise. Once
you have a large file, you will be able to create a suitable "Reaction
Sheet" to introduce or complete a topic in your current events
class. You may even wish to make up your own, presenting an
extremely controversial point of view.

Social Studies Activity #2: New Planet

FOCUS:
An important goal of social studies is to understand that a person's
value decisions are not immune to cultural influences. This activity
gives students a chance to plan alternative social structures and to
examine their priorities as they make decisions.

MATERIALS:
A "New Planet List" for each student.

PROCEDURE:
The students imagine they are establishing a society on a new
planet. They decide between a set of extreme alternatives and
establish a model for their culture. Students can then evaluate their
decisions in terms of their own environment on earth.

DIRECTIONS:
1. Give students the "New Planet List" to read.
2. Divide the class into groups of three or four.
3. Have each group make decisions listed in the "New Planet
List" and explain those decisions to the class.
4. Have the class as a whole relate their decisions to our world
today by considering the consequences for modern America.

New Planet List
You are in charge of the New Planet, looked upon as a possible
answer to Earth's overpopulation problems. Before New Planet,
similar in environment to Earth, can be inhabited, many decisions
must be made regarding its society and culture. Your task is to make
the decisions, in full agreement with your group. All members must
agree on answers to the following questions:
1. Will there be population control or no population control?
   If you choose population control, the planet will never be over-

populated and conditions will be much more pleasant. There will be more for everyone and life will be more enjoyable. However, the government will determine who can have children and how many they may have. There will be stiff penalties for the birth of unlicensed children. If you choose to have no population control, the government will have no say in the family decisions of whether to have children or not. There might, however, be overpopulation and all the problems that go with it in a thousand years.

2. Will there be naturally grown food or will it be created by chemical and artificial means?

If the food is grown naturally, it will be healthy and tasty. There will be less chance of diseases that result from chemical and artificial processing. But there will be less food produced and everyone will have to eat less. If food is produced artificially, there will be more than enough for all; however, it will taste rather bland and uninteresting. It will also not be as healthy for people as organic food.

3. Will the government be run by a single authority, such as a king or dictator, or will it be a democracy run by and for the people?

If the society is run by one individual, he will be the wisest and best able to deal with problems because of his great skill in governing. He will have the best staff possible to aid in his decisions. He will have absolute power to make the rules. If the government is determined by popular vote, no one individual will have absolute power and all decisions will be decided by popular vote. The best decisions might not be made, but all individuals in society will have an equal voice.

4. Will there be industrialism or no industrialism?

If there is industrialism, there will be many consumer goods for all. The land will be torn up for raw materials and there will be pollution problems. There might be an energy crisis eventually as fuels become used up. If there is no industrialism, there will be no mass-produced materials and everything will be made by hand. It will take longer to accomplish nearly everything, but the land will remain beautiful and there will be no shortage of energy. Pollution will not be a problem.

5. Will there be advanced methods of transportation or will the different communities be isolated?

With transportation systems, there will be a potential fuel crisis and a possible pollution problem. The natural landscape will be torn up for roads, parking lots, airports, train tracks and stations. Noise will also be a problem. If there is no structured transportation system, each colony will be isolated from the other. People will have trouble getting to stores and hospitals. It will be difficult for people in different colonies to visit one another.

6. Will there be a uniform culture or many subcultures?

If there is a uniform culture, everyone will be alike. There will be no diversity and no threat from groups who want to change things. There will be no bigotry, and society will run smoothly. If there are different cultures there will be diversity, and each culture will be able to learn from the other cultures. There will be the possibility of change—life will be dynamic. There will also be a chance for prejudice and conflict to arise in the different cultures.

7. Will formal education be compulsory or will each child and family have free choice about going to school?

If school is mandatory, all children will have to go to a state-controlled or approved school. There will be no exceptions. Everyone will receive the same education. If there is free choice in education, then each family will be able to decide on what kind of education their children will receive. The quality of education will be uneven.

8. Will there be equal supplies and materials for all or will some get more while others get less?

If everyone gets the same amount, no one will go hungry or be in need. Those who work the hardest will earn the same amount as those who don't work at all. If each person gets only what he earns, there will be inequities in the amount of goods that each person gets. There may be poor people who go hungry while the rich may have more than they can use.

9. Will there be guns for everyone or no one?

If everyone has a gun, each person will have an equal chance in times of danger. Hunting will be easier and sport shooting will be allowed. If no one has a gun, no one will be shot. Hunting will be more difficult, and there will be no sport shooting.

10. Will there be government files on every individual or no files on anyone at all?

If there are files on individuals, it will be easy to keep track of criminals and those who don't pay their debts. Any time a government official wants or needs to find information on a citizen, he will be able to just check the file and find out what he wants to know. Employers and other people will be able to get file information if the government believes there is good reason. If there are no files, it will be more difficult for the government to keep track of the deviant elements of society. But under this system, every citizen will have his privacy and no one's rights will be abused.

QUESTIONS FOR DISCUSSION:
1. How are these decisions reflected in our society?

2. How do we make these decisions in our country? In other countries?

3. How did you make the decisions in your group? What model for decision making did you use?

4. How can you apply your decisions to your life as it is now?

Science Activity #1: Crush the Can

FOCUS:

When air is removed from a can and a vacuum is created, the can is crushed by the forces surrounding it. Often, metaphorically, we are crushed by the forces surrounding us. This activity teaches students the concept of pressure and its effects as both a scientific phenomenon and a human experience.

MATERIALS:

A one-gallon metal can with screw-on cap, water, hot plate or other similar heating source.

PROCEDURE:

The students are to observe a metal can collapsing from air pressure, and make observations regarding it. Then, they are to apply what they have learned to human situations.

DIRECTIONS:

1. Ask the students to watch the procedure carefully.
2. Fill the one-gallon can one-eighth full of water.
3. Boil the water.
4. Shut off heat.
5. Put the lid on the can very tightly.
6. Watch the can collapse.

QUESTIONS FOR DISCUSSION:

1. What was the initial state of the can and its contents?
2. What happened next?
3. Did anything leave the can? What, if anything?
4. What is left of the can? Why?
5. How did it happen?
6. Do you ever feel crushed?
7. What do you feel like when you are crushed?
8. What do you lose when you are crushed?
9. How can you be restored? Can the can be restored?

Science Activity #2: Observation and Inference

FOCUS:

This activity gives the students a chance to recognize the differences between observation and inference in both natural and human phenomena.

MATERIALS:
Part of an engine, such as a crankshaft, a bobbin, the top of a baster, an old potato masher, an Allen wrench, a nail set, a cotter pin, styrofoam packing material, a glass cutter and an old style collar fastener. (This is only a sample set of materials—any collection of unfamiliar items will do.)

PROCEDURE:
Students will examine a series of unfamiliar objects; they will determine their functions by making observations and then inferences about the observations. They will then try the same procedure as they observe unfamiliar human behavior to determine what the behavior means.

DIRECTIONS:
1. Arrange the class in a semicircle with a table at the open end.
2. Place one of the unfamiliar objects on the table. If a student knows what the object is used for, he should disqualify himself.
3. As a group, have the students determine the purpose of the object, using the following procedure:

A student says, "I see . . . ." and makes one observation about the object to the class. If the observation is accurate, let him continue. If it's not, don't let him proceed. If he can go on he says, "And I imagine . . . ." For example: Bobbin—"I see that it is round." "I imagine that it turns like a wheel." He finishes his observation with a guess as to what the object is used for, using his original observation as a clue. Tell the class whether or not his assumption is true. If not, the class must disallow it as a possibility; if it is true, then it can be used as an observable fact and another person can make an assumption from it. Explain that students must listen very carefully to what other class members have said. This will aid them in their guesses.

4. This procedure is followed until the use of the object is discovered. It is important that you give no clues, and continue until the class finds the correct answer.
5. The activity may be repeated, about once a week, with different objects until students develop skill in making observations and drawing inferences about the observations.
6. Try the same procedure with a human interaction problem and give the students a chance to use what they have learned. The following are possible situations you may use. The task is for the students who are observers to discover what the students who are actors have done.

a. Have two students intently stare at each other for two or three minutes, pretending they are blind and listening for sounds.

They should pretend to be unaware that they are looking at each other. Have the class use the "I see . . . . I imagine . . . . " formula to discover what they are actually doing.

b. Unnoticed by the rest of the class, give a student a watch. Have him sit in the front of the class, reading or thumbing through a magazine, constantly twitching the arm wearing the watch in a very nervous fashion. The class probably will assume that he is nervous or afraid. Actually, he has a self-winding watch that he is trying to wind as he waits. Have the class use the "I see . . . . I imagine . . . . " formula to discover what he is really doing.

QUESTIONS FOR DISCUSSION:

1. Which is harder to make observations about, objects or people?

2. Which is harder to make inferences about, objects or people?

3. What happens when you are wrong in your observation about an object?

4. What happens when you are wrong in your inference about an object?

5. What happens when you are wrong about your observation about a person?

6. What happens when you are wrong about your inference about a person?

7. How can you make more accurate observations?

8. How can you make sure your inferences are true?

9. How can you make sure you are not confusing an inference with an observation?

FOOTNOTE:

It is essential for students to learn that inferences often appear as observations, and that it is dangerous to confuse the two. This activity will clearly demonstrate the differences. As other examples occur spontaneously in class, be sure to point them out to students.

Math Activity #1: Learning Catalogue

FOCUS:

An important reason for learning mathematical concepts is to become a better manager of time, money and affairs. In this activity, students are given a chance to order priorities using basic computation skills.

MATERIALS:

A "Learning Catalogue" for each student.

PROCEDURE:

Each student is given 100 units with which they may buy as much as possible from the "Learning Catalogue." Each item in the catalogue involves a certain amount of hours and each student has only 100 hours to use. The students must figure out how to get the most for their units in the time allowed.

DIRECTIONS:

1. Have each student compute what he wants to buy from the catalogue, making sure he does not spend over 100 units or 100 hours.

2. Have the students share their choices and their reasons for choices with the class.

Learning Catalogue

The following is a list of 25 things that you can learn to do. You may spend up to 100 units purchasing any of the items on the list, but you can only have 100 hours. Choose wisely and get the most of what you really want for your time and money.

Things to Learn	Units	Hours
1. How to play baseball	20	20
2. How to read better	40	30
3. How to be a great cook	60	10
4. How to be in perfect physical condition	60	50
5. How to improve your math ability	25	25
6. How to be a perfect son or daughter	70	65
7. How to be a good friend	75	60
8. How to prepare for any job you want	70	50
9. How to be a great dancer	30	10
10. How to be a better swimmer	15	25
11. How to make models	5	10
12. How to be a good artist	10	10
13. How to get baby-sitting jobs	30	5
14. How to get part-time jobs in the neighborhood	30	10

15. How to get all your teachers to like you a lot	30	30
16. How to design your own clothes	10	20
17. How to ride a horse	10	10
18. How to be a good ice skater	15	10
19. How to make a garden	15	10
20. How to develop a warm smile	50	25
21. How to train animals	30	30
22. How to arrange your time so that you can have more time for what you want	50	65
23. How to be more popular	75	60
24. How to be a good chess player	15	15
25. How to play a musical instrument of your choice	10	20

FOOTNOTE:

The activity can be adapted for more advanced students by incorporating more complex mathematical procedures. The students might enjoy making their own catalogue. Each student can put two or three catalogue items in a box and ask the teacher to put together a catalogue. Catalogues do not have to be "Learning" catalogues, but can be based on any subject of the students' or your own choosing. You might want to provide the students with 100 units in toothpicks or marbles to enable them to visualize the business transaction.

Math Activity #2: Value Word Problems

FOCUS:

We often present students with word problems to give mathematical computations contextual meaning, and to make computations realistic and interesting. You can invent problems that develop mathematic skills while giving students a chance to consider value questions that actually apply to life. This activity suggests problems that have proven to be both meaningful and challenging to students.

MATERIALS:

Samples of word problems (see below).

PROCEDURE:

Present word problems to the class as you would any math word problem. Discussion of answers can follow. Here are four examples of different value word problems.

1. You get $1 a week for doing chores that take ten hours a week of your time, and your younger brother gets 50 cents a week for doing one hour's worth of chores. How much do you get an hour? How much does your brother get an hour? Is your rate of pay fair? How do you feel about the fact that your younger brother gets a different

rate of pay? How much allowance do you think you should get for ten hours of work? How much is that per hour?

2. You have a job calling people on the phone and telling them about a special sale at a nearby store. You get paid five cents a call but cannot receive more than $5. There is no way that the owner of the store can check on the number of calls you make. If you actually make 75 calls, how much do you earn? If you cheated and said that you earned all of the $5, how many calls must you claim? How many calls will you actually claim? Why? How much more can you get by lying? Is it worth it to you?

3. Your mother bought you a $50 tricycle when you were four years old. You are now eight years old and you want a new bicycle. The trike is being used by your younger sister. Your father says that he will pay for half of a new bike, which costs $80, but you must pay the other half. How much of your own money will you need? The bike store will take your trike in trade; the owner will take off $10 from the original price for the first year of age and $3 for every year after that. How much will he give you for your old tricycle? Do you think it is a fair price? If you sell the trike to the store, your sister will have no trike and your mother will have to buy her one. Your mother says the decision is yours. Will you sell it? If you sell it, how much more will you still have to earn? What ways can you earn that much money? How long will it take you to get the amount you need? Do you think it's right for you to sell a bike that was a gift to you, knowing that the person who bought the gift will have to spend more money because of what you're now doing?

4. Every day after school you have three hours before supper; this time is yours to do with as you please. You can play ball, have a paper route, join a school club or take part in any one of several activities. If you play ball, it will take up the entire time. If you have the paper route, it will take two hours and your other hour will be free. The school club takes one hour. You can collect for the community fund for one to two hours. You can do homework for one and a half hours and be able to watch TV after supper for one and a half hours. You can play with a friend who can only spend one hour with you. How will you spend your time? What percent of your time would be spent on each activity?

FOOTNOTE:
You can convert any word problem into a value problem by combining the calculations and mathematical procedures with questions concerning why a student needs to learn math and what he might use it for in his life. Remember, all value questions must have "you" for the subject.

5
CREATING ACTIVITIES FOR YOUR CLASSROOM

While this book and the many others listed in our resource section should help you launch and maintain a successful value clarification program, the most effective and personally rewarding activities are those you and your students will create. Most likely you have already adapted activities in this handbook to your own unique situation and students. The step-by-step process described in this chapter will help you go one step further and create your own activities. It is not necessary to exactly follow the procedure nor to use it as a fixed, rigid formula. Use it instead as a set of fluid guidelines that may spark your own creativity.

A. Choosing A Topic

In choosing a topic, be it either confluent or affective, talk with your students to find out what is important to them. It is imperative that the topic selected be appropriate for your students. A lively, creative unit about buying and choosing clothes that represents students' feelings is certainly inappropriate for students whose parents buy all their clothes. Your topic must serve the students you teach. If you have a fixed curriculum or you wish to use the third level teaching model, begin by asking yourself:

1. Why is it important that someone learn this material?
2. What difference will it make in their lives?
3. How might someone better understand himself as a result of learning this material?

Having arrived at a general topic, your next concern is to focus in on the central issue. Look for causes rather than symptoms. For example, a curriculum that deals directly with the central issues is a "drug unit" that does not explain the dangers of drugs, but rather helps students understand loneliness, peer pressure, alienation and powerlessness. These concerns cause the drug problem in the first place, so it makes sense to build activities that deal directly with them.

B. Selecting Valuing Processes

Now you will have to decide which steps in the valuing process your activity will include; generally, a single activity cannot cover *all* steps simultaneously.

Each activity grows out of one or more of these processes. For example, to encourage students to examine different alternatives, an activity may present various choices and allow the students to select from them. An activity based primarily on the process of acting may ask the students to inventory past actions for a month or require them to try acting in a new way that is more consistent with one of their values.

Suppose, for example, your topic is pollution. The inventorying activity might ask students to list all the things they did to help the environment during the last month—picking up papers, telling others to pick up papers, asking parents to buy nonpolluting soap, walking to a place that was safe and close instead of driving. Trying a new behavior might include any of the above acts that the students have never done. Other possibilities are distributing information in the neighborhood or volunteering to work at a recycling center.

Write down the steps in the valuing process which will be included in your activity as Item B in your planning outline. Here you can see a model based on the topic we use for illustration.

A. Sample Topic:	Doing What I Admire
B. Values Processes:	Choosing freely, choosing from alternatives, prizing, acting

C. Outlining Objectives

Your next step will be to state objectives for your planned activity. What do you want your students to gain from it? What experiences do you want them to have? Two kinds of objectives go into developing a value clarification activity. First are the cognitive objectives which most teachers have worked with in other teaching situations. Remember that cognitive objectives state behavioral outcomes. When designing your activities, you must identify and list the specific behavioral outcomes that are appropriate.

Affective objectives differ from cognitive objectives in that they stress the structure of the experience or the process, rather than the outcome of the activity. It is unfair and impossible, we feel, to predict exact outcomes for activities in value clarification. Instead you can introduce a process which you want students to experience. The results may be as varied as are the individual students. These objectives cannot be measured as predictable, observable behaviors, but they help the teacher guide students through an activity.

Write down your objectives for a planned activity. Here you can see samples of both cognitive and affective objectives.

A. Sample Topic:	Doing What I Admire
B. Values Processes:	Choosing freely, choosing from alternatives, prizing, acting

C. Objectives:
Cognitive:
1. List five heroes.
2. List three actions that are admirable for each hero.
Affective:
1. Determine two new behaviors for yourself that are admirable, and try them out.
2. Report back to class on your progress.

D. Deciding Where to Focus

Now that you have chosen a topic, objectives and valuing processes, you are well on the road to creating a specific activity. You must now determine the specific focal points of the activity. Alternatives to consider are:

1. The activity can relate to the past, present or future.
2. The activity can be either experiential, experimental or thinking and reflecting. Experiential means that the students try a new behavior or a new set of behaviors in their real lives and see the result. Experimental means they try it in a controlled environment such as role-playing in a small support group. Thinking and reflecting means the students consider how they live without actually doing the specific action.
3. The activity can be done in a large group, small group or individually. It can also be done in a combination of the three.

Write down your areas of focus once you have decided which ones fit your activity and students.

A. Sample Topic:	Doing What I Admire
B. Values Processes:	Choosing freely, choosing from alternatives, prizing, acting
C. Objectives:	
Cognitive:	1. List five heroes.
	2. List three actions that are admirable for each hero.
Affective:	1. Determine two new behaviors for yourself that are admirable, and try them out.
	2. Report back to class on your progress.
D. Focuses:	Present, future
	Reflection, experiential
	Individual, large group

E. Putting It All Together — The Procedure

The activity format is now complete. You have only to design specific steps for the students to follow. The suggestions below come from our own experiences working with a variety of classes.

1. When you present alternatives to the students for them to choose, make sure that each alternative is equally appealing or unappealing. The more difficult the choice, the better the activity.
2. Make the activities fun and as interesting as possible. Dress them up with interesting stories and personally involving situations. This does not mean they are frivolous, but rather presented in a dramatic, meaningful way.
3. Make sure the directions are clear and manageable. It's helpful to try the activity yourself or with family or friends before doing it with your students.
4. Use as much movement and group sharing as possible. This keeps the students from getting too bogged down in serious thought. Reflection is good, but young children have short attention spans.
5. Try to include as much of the students' real world as possible. Encourage them to practice anything that they discover in terms of new behaviors. Also use real life examples that students can relate to.
6. Process the activity by using one of the techniques described in Chapter 6. Or, if time allows, make up your own. Use your objectives as a guide to develop a processing or evaluating step that logically grows out of the students' learning experience.
7. Change the activity as you go along if you discover that it needs modification. It often takes more than one try to get an activity just right, so don't give up too quickly if it doesn't seem to work.

Write down your procedure, step by step. This is most important when you have relatively little experience in creating activities, or when directions are complex. Be flexible enough to modify procedures, to clarify the activity or to help confused students.

A. Sample Topic:	Doing What I Admire
B. Values Processes:	Choosing freely, choosing from alternatives, prizing, acting
C. Objectives:	
Cognitive:	1. List five heroes.
	2. List three actions that are admirable for each hero.
Affective:	1. Determine two new behaviors for yourself that are admirable, and try them out.
	2. Report back to class on your progress.

D. Focuses:	Present, future Reflection, experiential Individual, large group

E. Procedure:	1. Each student lists five heroes from television, books, movies or real life. They must be heroes that the student truly admires.
	2. List three actions that each hero does that make him admirable. There are fifteen actions, though some may be repeated.
	3. Code the fifteen items as follows:
	    Yes—I do it already.
	    No—I don't intend to do it.
	    Will try—I don't do it, but I want to try it.
	4. Each student chooses two items from the last category and tries them in the next two weeks.
	5. After two weeks, each student reports to the class as a whole on their progress in doing the two actions.

Remember that our procedure for creating activities is only a model to be used as long as it works for you. Sometimes you will start where we did with Item A, Choosing A Topic, but other times you will begin at another point on the outline and build from there. After considerable experience, you may never consciously separate the developmental steps outlined on the model. However, if at any time your activities seem to be ineffective or lacking direction, this model may make them clear and workable again.

The model does not guarantee an endless supply of creative ideas; your own creativity will be the best source for new activities. Listen to your students. Follow the leads they reveal in conversations inside and outside the classroom. Consider current classroom, school-wide and community situations as rich sources for new topics. Any controversy has potential as a topic for value clarification activities. If value clarification becomes integral to your teaching, you will devise new activities and adapt old ones in a spiral, generating from your creativity and, in turn, feeding it.

6
EVALUATING, RECORD KEEPING AND PROCESSING

Can you evaluate students' work in value clarification, a process where there are no right or wrong answers, where students always have the right to "pass" and where participation in activities is voluntary? We believe evaluation is not only possible but essential if students are to gain significant and lasting learning from their effort.

Self-Evaluation

The primary responsibility for evaluation rests with the student himself. All evaluation techniques should include the type of processing in which students ask themselves questions to determine how their experiences in different activities have changed them, and what meaning they see in their new discoveries.

Youngsters of all ages can evaluate their own experiences, and it is helpful for them to begin self-evaluation at an early age. They are the best authorities on what they have learned in value clarification. The teacher's responsibility in the evaluation process is to facilitate self-evaluation by providing opportunities for it to take place and supplying appropriate tools and mechanisms.

In confluent or third level teaching, evaluation devices such as tests or grades can be used to determine right or wrong answers for some of the material. But you must take great care to avoid disasterous results for the entire unit if you choose these traditional tools of evaluation. Suppose you give grades for the part of the curriculum which is based on public knowledge—the facts, concepts and learnings which can be tested. By grading or giving teacher evaluations to one part of the unit but not to the other, you will communicate to students, either implicitly or explicitly, that the two areas are unconnected. This will, in turn, suggest to students that the affective and cognitive domains are separate. However, the reason for using the confluent approach is to stress connections between the two domains. Thus you may end up teaching the opposite of your original intention by using self-evaluation for one part and teacher evaluations for the other. Furthermore, students invariably assume that the teacher-evaluated part is more important than the student-evaluated part; they tend to see the affective or value clarification activities as games, while the "real learning" takes place in the cognitive activities. This phenomenon occurs most often in higher grades after children are conditioned to teacher evaluations.

You can avoid this problem by encouraging students to self-evaluate all aspects of the confluent curriculum. If you wish to assess cognitive learnings in a confluent lesson to check progress and meet individual needs of the students, do so diagnostically, not judgmentally. You will destroy the potential for learning by using judgmental evaluations.

Central Questions

Many different types of self-evaluation methods can be used, but each method ultimately leads students to answer the following questions:
1. What have I learned?
2. How does this learning affect my life?
3. What choices have I made?
4. What are the consequences of those choices?
5. What options are open for me?
6. Where do I go from here?

The Journal

A journal is a good place for students to keep an ongoing record of their progress. A journal is similar to a personal diary and might be shared, in part, from time to time. Entries can include a record of the value clarification activities, any written responses to them, how the students felt doing the activity and what the activity meant to them. Students can examine this record periodically to discover answers to the central questions above. Listed below are a number of methods to help structure the students' journal entries.
1. *"I Learned Statements."* The student completes sentences telling what he has learned about himself by doing an activity.
   a. "I learned that I . . . ."
   b. "I relearned that I . . . ."
   c. "I discovered that I . . . ."
   d. "I found that I . . . ."
   e. "I felt good when I . . . ."
   f. "I was proud that I . . . ."
   g. "I was disappointed that I . . . ."

"I Learned Statements" can be used at the end of an activity when students reflect on the personal learning the activity had for them. The second "I" is most important because self-knowledge is the most significant aspect of value clarification.

2. *Open-Ended Sentences.* These are similar to "I Learned Statements" but cover a much wider area of inquiry. Because open-ended sentences are more structured, they might work better with younger children than "I Learned Statements."

    a. "It was fun for me when I . . . ."
    b. "I enjoyed doing . . . because . . . ."
    c. "I was embarrassed when I . . . because . . . ."
    d. "I wish I had . . . ."
    e. "It made me nervous when . . . ."
    f. "Next time I will . . . ."
    g. "I got angry when . . . ."
    h. "I was bored when . . . ."
    i. "I liked it when . . . ."
    j. "I want to learn more about . . . ."
    k. "I want to try . . . ."
    l. "If given another chance I would . . . ."
    m. "I felt . . . when . . . ."

You can adapt "I Learned Statements" and open-ended sentences for younger children who have difficulty articulating responses. Use picture completions or supply a list of alternative responses (either pictures or words) for the student to circle when completing the sentence. For example:

At the end of the activity I felt . . . .

happy   sad   eyes open   eyes closed
                                   learned much   learned little

3. *Self-Contracts.* Self-contracts are similar to New Year's resolutions but require stronger commitment. After an activity where students decide to try a new behavior, they write that behavior in the form of a self-contract. Later, they keep a record of their progress in fulfilling the self-contract. This evaluation method helps students translate their learning into action. The most effective self-contracts state planned behavior and are concise and to the point. A useful form is "I will . . . by . . . and know that I have done so by . . . ." The self-contract "I will be friendly" is not as effective

as the self-contract "I will smile today," because the first is too vague. Self-contracts should be stated in positive terms. Say what *will* be done, not what *will not* be done. For example, a poor self-contract would be "I will not argue with my sister for a week;" a good self-contract would be "I will agree with my sister for a week." Students will have a hard time evaluating self-contracts that are stated in negative terms.

4. *Continua.* Here students evaluate experiences by marking a place on a line. Any continuum used in self-evaluation forces students to take a stand on what they have learned. Some examples of continua are shown here.

Mark your position on the following lines:

paid no attention during the activity
⎣_____|_____⎦
paid strict attention during the activity

paid attention only when it was my turn

it was difficult to answer questions honestly
⎣_____|_____⎦
it was easy to answer questions honestly

trusted no one in my group
⎣_____|_____⎦
trusted everyone in my group

never talked at all
⎣_____|_____⎦
talked all the time

talked only when asked to

because _____
_____

learned nothing new about myself
⎣_____|_____⎦
learned 10 new things about myself

because _____
_____

```
am just like                            am very different from
other students                              the other students
    └─────────────────────────────────────────────────────┘
                        am like about
                        half the students
    because _____
    _____

    acted in brand                              acted just like
    new ways                                      I always do
        └───────────────────────────────────────────────────┘
    because _____
    _____

    I was silly                                   I was serious
        └───────────────────────────────────────────────────┘
```

Students can create their own continua once they have had
experience using some. You can ask students to create a number of
continua for use in their journals and to share newly created
continua with the whole class.

5. *Thought/Feeling Charts.* These charts help students separate
their thoughts and feelings. Any format may be used for the charts,
but we suggest the following models:

A. Thoughts/Feelings Chart
1. Have students draw a chart to keep in their journals.

2. After each activity, provide time for students to add reactions
   to the chart.

3. Encourage periodic analysis of this cumulative record.

DATE	ACTIVITY	I THINK....	I FEEL....

B. Two-sided Coin

1. Make coins from cardboard or stiff paper.

2. Students note date or activity name on coin.

3. Students record on one side their *thoughts* about the activity; on the other side, their *feelings*.

4. Students keep all "coins" in a thought/feeling bank.

5. After accumulating many coins, students may examine them periodically to look for patterns in their learning.

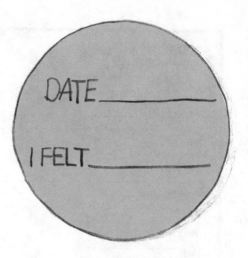

As in all evaluation activities, it is the accumulation of thoughts and feelings over time that furnishes the most insight. Students can look for patterns in their lives and for possible self-contracts to emerge from the records they keep.

Long-Term Projects

Another type of self-evaluation is sharing a long-term project with the whole class. Here a student can synthesize thoughts and feelings about a project with encouragement and assistance from the class. The project presentation is a public activity, whereas a journal is primarily private. This procedure allows students to incorporate the value processes of acting and acting repeatedly on their beliefs. Most activities described earlier in this handbook can become the basis of a long-term project. Or you can suggest other long-term projects like the one below to fit current interests of students.

A student discovers that he values friendship and decides to do a long-term project to improve the quality of his friendships. He sends brief notes to each of his friends after school, sharing any important part of his day. He makes inexpensive but thoughtful presents and sends them to each friend once a week for two months. He prepares a "friendship survey" and gives it to his friends to find out what their likes and dislikes are (things he might not have previously known). After a couple of months he shares with the class what he attempted to do, his methods and what he learned about himself and his friendships as a result of the project.

In doing a long-term project, the students might use any or all of the evaluation techniques used in journal keeping. The project can be as sophisticated or simple as the class needs dictate. Remind students that the project will be shared and not to include in the public presentation anything that is too personal.

Whatever method of self-evaluation students choose, remember that all activities do not mean the same thing to all students. Do not feel discouraged by negative or apathetic responses on the part of some students; these are just as valid as positive, supportive responses. Regardless of the outcome, students will still have profited by experiencing the activity. Often, changes in personal meaning occur over time, and value clarification changes are not immediately apparent. Of course, if a majority of students gain nothing from an activity, then, perhaps, the activity was inappropriate for them.

The important goal to keep in mind for evaluation activities is to provide continuous and varied experiences to help students incorporate the valuing process into their lives. The evaluation of value clarification activities gives students time to understand what they are learning, and tools to evaluate their own progress and the meaning they see in their progress.

7
RESOURCES —
BOOKS AND ARTICLES

Some of the books and articles on this list explain, amplify or clarify the ideas and philosophy behind humanistic education and value clarification; others provide you with more examples of curricula, activities and strategies to use with your students. The comments that follow summarize the main thrust of each resource.

1. Abramowitz, Mildred, and Claudia Macari. "Values Clarification in Junior High School," *Educational Leadership*, vol. 29, no. 7 (April 1972).
An article by two inner city junior high administrators who taught a course in value clarification. It explains how the course was set up, what activities were used and the effects of the course on students.

2. "An Exchange of Opinion," *Learning Magazine*, vol.1, no.2 (December 1972).
Sidney Simon and Lawrence Kohlberg have different opinions on moral and values education. This article is a dialogue between them.

3. Association for Supervision and Curriculum Development. *Perceiving, Behaving, Becoming: A New Focus for Education.* Washington, D.C.: ASCD, 1962.
Edited by Art Combs, this book is a landmark in the theory and practice of humanistic education. Although it does not apply directly to the classroom, the material is enlightening for all teachers.

4. Borton, Terry. *Reach, Touch and Teach: Student Concerns and Process Education.* New York: McGraw-Hill, 1970.
Terry Borton helped run the summer project in Philadelphia which is described in this book. It presents a useful model for the teaching of all humanistic education and eloquently describes the interaction between the author and his students.

Useful activities are also described.

5. Brown, George Isaac. *Human Teaching for Human Learning: An Introduction to Confluent Education.* New York: Viking, 1971.
Brown describes the theory and a clear model of confluent education. The book is filled with practical activities for converting a class into a model of confluent education.

6. Castillo, Gloria. *Left-Handed Teaching: Lessons in Affective Education.* New York: Praeger, 1974.
A handy book that describes most of the standard affective activities. Although there is repetition from other sources, the book catalogues many activities and makes a good reference guide.

7. Curwin, G. et al. *Search for Values.* Dayton, Ohio: Pflaum/ Standard, 1972.
This package is a total curriculum for high school value clarification. Designed for older students, it is easily adaptable for students of all ages. Themes include units in authority, competition, commitment, personal space, images, relationships and time. Included are spirit masters and a teacher's handbook.

8. Curwin, Richard, and Barbara Fuhrmann. "Is Your Teaching What You Think It Is?", *Learning Magazine,* (Part I, April 1974, Part II, May/June, 1974).
These articles present activities to help teachers understand their priorities in teaching, and to help them discover if their actual classroom behaviors reflect their priorities.

9. Curwin, Richard, and Barbara Fuhrmann. *Discovering Your Teaching Self: Humanistic Approaches to Effective Teaching.* Englewood Cliffs, N.J.: Prentice-Hall, 1975.
A complete program for becoming an effective teacher. This book gives a model and many activities for becoming aware of your values, goals, self-perceptions and past experiences as they relate to your teaching. It also provides many methods for gaining awareness of your teaching behaviors. All of the activities have application for use with students.

10. Elder, Carl A. *Making Value Judgments: Decisions for Today.*

Columbus, Ohio: Charles E. Merrill Co., 1972.
A book designed for high school students as a text for understanding the valuing process. A teacher's handbook is also available. Many of the activities can be used with junior high students.

11. Fraenkel, Jack R. *Helping Students to Think and Value, Strategies for Teaching The Social Studies.* Englewood Cliffs, N.J.: Prentice-Hall, 1973.
A cognitive view of teaching the social studies with a focus on thinking and valuing. Much of the book is explanation of the author's model, and there are curriculum suggestions to augment the theoretical framework.

12. Gibson, John. *The Intergroup Relations Curriculum: A Program For Elementary School Education*, vol.2. Lincoln Filene Center for Citizenship and Public Affairs, Tufts University, 1969.
Loaded with good activities for helping elementary students gain awareness and experience in intergroup relations.

13. Ginott, Haim. *Teacher and Child.* New York: Macmillan, 1972.
A book that presents the noted psychologist-educator's views on the psychology of building positive self-concepts. It is an excellent guide for dealing with everyday problems that occur in the classroom. The delightful anecdotes help illustrate such topics as discipline, praise, communication, cooperation and trust.

14. Glasser, William. *Schools Without Failure.* New York: Harper & Row, 1969.
An explanation of the theory behind schools that are effective without the threat of failure. Many examples illustrate the model. It is a helpful guide for building a classroom without threat.

15. Gray, Farnum. "Doing Something About Values," *Learning Magazine*, vol. 1, no. 2 (December 1972).
A description of a two day value clarification workshop conducted by Sidney Simon. The author shares his feelings, concerns and insights into the process.

16. Greer, Mary, and Bonnie Rubinstein. *Will the Real Teacher Please Stand Up: A Primer in Humanistic Education.* Paci-

fic Palisades, Calif.: Goodyear Publishing Co., 1972.
A collection of reprints from books, articles and student writings that applies to the genera! theme of humanistic education. It offers a well-rounded view of humanistic education.

17. Harmin, Merrill, Howard Kirschenbaum and Sidney Simon. *Clarifying Values Through Subject Matter.* Minneapolis: Winston Press, 1973.
The authors give examples from nearly every subject and age level of how to clarify values and teach subject matter congruently. The book does not go into depth about any one subject, but scans many. It explains the model of third level teaching.

18. Harmin, Merrill, Howard Kirschenbaum and Sidney Simon. "Teaching Science With a Focus on Values," *The Science Teacher*, vol. 37, no. 1 (January 1970).
An article that explains how science can be taught with a focus on values; gives a rationale for doing so.

19. Harmin, Merrill, Howard Kirschenbaum and Sidney Simon. "The Search for Values With a Focus on Math," *Teaching Mathematics In The Elementary School: What's Needed? What's Happening?* Washington, National Association of Elementary School Principals and National Council of Teachers of Mathematics (1970), pp. 81–89.
This article gives examples of teaching elementary math and value clarification simultaneously, and reasons for teaching this way.

20. Harmin, Merrill, and Sidney Simon. "The Subject Matter Controversy Revisited," *Peabody Journal Of Education*, vol. 42, no. 4 (January 1965), pp. 194–205.
This is one of the first articles describing the third level teaching model. The authors explain the model and how it applies to different subject areas. Examples are provided.

21. Harmin, Merrill, and Sidney Simon. "Values and Teaching: A Humane Process," *Educational Leadership*, vol. 24, no. 6 (March 1967), pp. 517–525.
This article includes different activities that teachers can use to help their students clarify values.

22. Hawley, Robert, and Isabel Hawley. *A Handbook of Personal Growth Activities for Classroom Use.* Amherst, Mass.: ERA, 1972.
   An excellent handbook filled with personal growth and value clarification activities. The activities are designed for use with all students. The handbook is written in an easy-to-use fashion.

23. Hawley, Robert, Sidney Simon and David Britton. *Composition for Personal Growth.* New York: Hart, 1973.
   This book explains how to turn traditional composition lessons in English and language arts into meaningful activities that help build self-awareness and personal growth. The activities are very useful and adaptable for most English or language arts classes.

24. Holt, John. *How Children Fail.* New York: Dell, 1964.
   (See following description.)

25. Holt, John. *How Children Learn.* New York: Dell, 1972.
   Holt is an eloquent writer who shares his feelings about education in these two books. Written in a uniquely personal style, the books are filled with examples, anecdotes and questions of concern to all teachers.

26. Johnson, David W. *Reaching Out: Interpersonal Effectiveness and Self-Actualization.* Englewood Cliffs, N.J.: Prentice-Hall, 1972.
   A book of personal growth activities for use in the classroom. It is most helpful in outlining communication and self-disclosure techniques.

27. Jourard, Sidney. *The Transparent Self.* New York: Van Nostrand Reinhold Co., 1971.
   A psychologist's view of self-disclosure and how it helps individuals grow. Not all of the chapters apply directly to teachers, but the book is worthwhile for anyone helping relationships.

28. Katz, Richard. *Preludes to Growth.* New York: The Free Press, 1973.
   Katz explains his view of the personal growth approach to education, and gives plenty of examples and activities to help the teacher understand the process.

29. Kirschenbaum, Howard, and Sidney Simon. "Teaching English with a Focus on Values," *The English Journal*, vol. 58, no. 7 (October 1969), pp. 1071–1076.
This article explains the need for teaching English with a focus on values. There are classroom examples to help the teacher understand the process.

30. Kirschenbaum, Howard, and Sidney Simon, eds. *Readings in Values Clarification*. Minneapolis: Winston Press, 1973.
A good collection of readings that pertains to the Raths model of value clarification. The readings cover a wide range of topics and have a very useful annotated bibliography.

31. Klein, Ronald et al. *Search for Meaning*. Dayton, Ohio: Pflaum/Standard, 1974.
A sequel to *Search for Values*, aimed at the junior high student. This is a curriculum package that includes activities, spirit masters and a teacher's handbook. The activities can be adapted for use with students of all ages. The units include external forces, internal drives and encounters.

32. Kohlberg, Lawrence. "The Child As A Moral Philosopher," *Psychology Today*, vol. 2, no. 4 (September 1968).
(See following description.)

33. Kohlberg, Lawrence, with Phillip Whitten. "Understanding the Hidden Curriculum," *Learning Magazine*, vol. 1, no. 2 (December 1972).
Kohlberg sees value development in sequential, natural stages, and these articles expand his model and theory. While Kohlberg's view is controversial, it helps clarify moral issues and education. He has done much research to back his view.

34. Krathwohl, David, Benjamin Bloom and Bertram Masia. *Taxonomy of Educational Objectives, Handbook 2: Affective Domain*. New York: McKay Co., 1964.
The authors have carefully delineated objectives in the affective domain and put them in rank order. While this book will not help a teacher in actual practice, it will structure concerns in the affective domain.

35. Marshall, Bernice. *Experiences in Being*. Monterey, Calif.: Brooks-Cole, 1971.

A collection of interesting readings about "being." The readings offer a broad view of what makes us human. One of the nicest aspects of this book is that it has a broader focus than just education.

36. Maslow, Abraham H. *Motivation and Personality.* 2nd ed. New York: Harper & Row, 1970.
Maslow's theory of personality is explained and defined in this interesting book. Maslow is one of the founders of the humanistic movement and his writings provide insights into what humanistic education is all about.

37. Maslow, Abraham H. *Toward a Psychology of Being.* 2nd ed. New York: Van Nostrand Reinhold Co., 1968.
Maslow presents his concept of humanistic psychology. This is heavy reading, but worth the effort. This book gives the basis for all the activities that so many other educators and psychologists have later developed.

38. Metcalf, Lawrence E., ed. *Values Education: Rationale, Strategies and Procedures.* Washington, D.C.: National Council for the Social Studies, 41st Yearbook, 1971.
Social studies has been one place in the traditional curriculum that has accepted responsibility for dealing with questions of values. The N.C.S.S. yearbook examines how this can best be accomplished, complete with activities and curriculum examples.

39. Neill, A. S. *Summerhill: A Radical Approach to Child Rearing.* New York: Hart, 1960.
Neill's vivid account of his now famous school, Summerhill. Neill's model for education is highly controversial and stimulating. The psychological implications for learning have application for most classrooms.

40. Otto, Herbert. *Group Methods to Actualize Human Potential: A Handbook.* National Center for Exploration of Human Potential, 976 Chalcedony St., San Diego, Calif. 92109.
A collection of activities, strategies and methods designed to help promote growth in human potential. There is a wide variety of activities, ranging from fantasy and touching exercises to communication skills. A very helpful collection.

41. Pfeiffer, J. William, and John E. Jones. *Handbook of Structured Experiences for Human Relations Training*, vol.1–3. University Associates, P.O. Box 615, Iowa City, Iowa 52240.
   Another collection of activities dealing with human relations. These handbooks clearly explain how to do a wide variety of activities. Most of the activities can be used or adapted for people of all ages.

42. Postman, Neil, and Charles Weingartner. *Teaching As a Subversive Activity*. New York: Dell, 1971.
   A radical approach to education that doesn't seem radical at all when the authors' proposals are given some thought. While the book focuses mostly on language, it is a valuable guide for all teachers who question what they are doing, and wish to share their questioning with two articulate critics of traditional education.

43. Raths, Louis, Merrill Harmin and Sidney Simon. *Values and Teaching*. Columbus, Ohio: Charles E. Merrill Co., 1966.
   The first major work that describes the value clarification process. The book focuses on the nature of valuing, how the process works and the applications for education. There are some activities and strategies that exemplify the basic points, along with a helpful chapter on guidelines and problems.

44. Raths, Louis, Merrill Harmin and Sidney Simon. "Helping Children Clarify Values," *NEA Journal*, vol. 56, no. 7 (October 1967), pp. 12–15.
   This article repeats the basic value clarification model and processes of valuing, and presents a few activities for classroom use.

45. Rogers, Carl R. *Freedom to Learn*. Columbus, Ohio: Charles E. Merrill Co., 1969.
   One of the most important and influential books in education. Rogers excites the readers with the potential of education for helping students and teachers grow. The vision of education in this book has had a profound effect on us.

46. Rokeach, Milton. *Beliefs, Attitudes, Values: A Theory of Organization and Change*. San Francisco: Jossey-Bass, 1968.
   Rokeach has put together a theoretical framework concerning beliefs, attitudes and values, explaining the differences in these

concepts, yet providing a conceptualization of how they all fit together into a cognitive view of how man functions at this level. He uses research to substantiate his views.

47. Rucker, W. Ray, V. Clyde Arnspiger and Arthur J. Brodbeck. *Human Values in Education.* Dubuque, Iowa: Kendall/Hunt, 1969.
A handy book that presents a model for teachers to use in applying values to the classroom. It has the basis of developing curricula, of experimenting and research. The most helpful parts of the book are probably the classroom examples.

48. Shaftel, Fannie R. and George Shaftel. *Role-Playing for Social Values: Decision-Making in the Social Studies.* Englewood Cliffs, N.J.: Prentice-Hall, 1967.
This book explains what role-playing is and how it can be used in the social studies class for dealing with questions of values. There is a theoretical discussion of social studies that is a helpful model for setting up role-playing in the classroom. There are many role-playing situations that are appropriate for the elementary classroom.

49. Silberman, Charles E. *Crisis in the Classroom.* New York: Random House, 1970.
A monumental book that illustrates the problems in education at all levels. While there are few solutions offered, Silberman backs up his claim of education being "mindless" with countless examples and evidence. After reading this book, classroom teachers will rethink their positions about much of what they are doing.

50. Simon, Sidney. "The Teacher Educator in Value Development," *Phi Delta Kappan*, vol. 53, no. 10 (June 1972), pp. 649-651.
This article makes a case for using value clarification in teacher education. There are examples of activities that exemplify the premise.

51. Simon, Sidney and Alice Carnes. "Teaching Afro-American History With a Focus on Values," *Educational Leadership*, vol. 27, no. 3 (December 1969), pp. 222–223.
Examples and a rationale of activities that illustrate how Afro-American history can be taught with a focus on value clarification. The examples are adaptable for the elementary classroom.

52. Simon, Sidney, and Merrill Harmin. "Subject Matter With a Focus on Values," Educational Leadership, vol. 26, no. 1 (October 1968), pp. 34–39.
An article that presents the third level teaching model. There are examples from various subjects on how to implement the model in the classroom.

53. Simon, Sidney, Leland Howe and Howard Kirschenbaum. Values Clarification: A Handbook Of Practical Strategies For Teachers And Students. New York: Hart, 1972.
A collection of most of the value clarification activities that have been presented in articles and books on value clarification, along with many new ones. The activities have application for all classrooms and students. A very useful book for developing curriculum in value clarification.

54. Weinstein, Gerald, and Mario D. Fantini, eds. Toward Humanistic Education: A Curriculum of Affect. New York: Praeger, 1970.
An excellent book that presents the "trumpet," a model for humanistic education. There are classroom examples of how to implement the trumpet. The book defines the purposes, goals and methods of humanistic education.